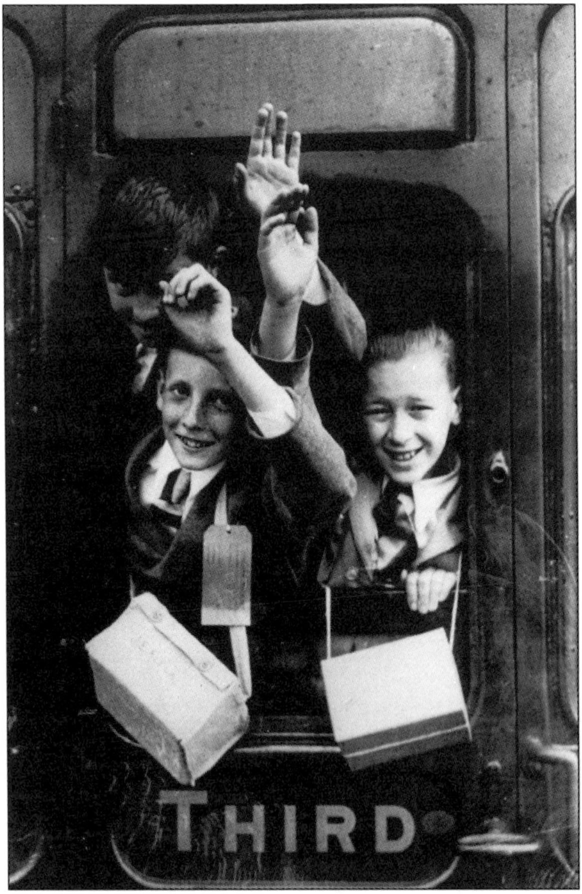
THIRD

With Schoolcap, Label and Cardboard Box

(Recollections of a World War Two Evacuee)

George Prager

*To Cliff,
with Best Wishes
George Prager*

The Pentland Press Limited
Edinburgh · Cambridge · Durham · USA

© George Prager 1999

First published in 1999 by
The Pentland Press Ltd.
1 Hutton Close
South Church
Bishop Auckland
Durham

All rights reserved.
Unauthorised duplication
contravenes existing laws.

British Library Cataloguing in Publication Data.
A catalogue record for this book is available
from the British Library.

ISBN 1 85821 714 8

Typeset by George Wishart & Associates, Whitley Bay.
Printed and bound by Antony Rowe Ltd., Chippenham.

Dedication

To Douglas and Muriel
and
In memory of Jennie and Tom Pritchard,
my wartime parents

The Countess Mountbatten of Burma.

Foreword

I am particularly pleased that George Prager has decided to write an account of the four most formative years of his life, aged 12 to 16, as one of the many wartime evacuee schoolchildren. His varied experiences ranged from being billeted with a film star in Kent to living in a mining valley in South Wales.

Most of his memories are good ones, unlike some of his contemporaries alas, and he seems to have coped well with the bad ones. But what shines through is that this young teenager approached the often-daunting new experiences determined to make the best of them and learning to be self-reliant at an early age. These characteristics must have served him well in later life.

George Prager's childhood experiences of some sixty years ago, as one of many children of a whole generation, make one wonder (with present-day better understanding of the importance of childhood influences) how most of them coped with the loneliness and homesickness suffered by so many, without being scarred for life. But this account shows us that with resilience and determination it *is* possible.

My own experiences as a teenage wartime evacuee to America make me very sensitive to the author's feelings. I am sure this account will bring back many memories for some readers, and be an eye-opener for others who never experienced the trauma of being an evacuee.

Patricia Mountbatten of Burma

Introduction

My local radio station, BBC Radio Kent, broadcast an appeal by Winnie Rolfe for memories and details of experiences of evacuees in World War Two, especially from Kent, to be sent to her. The information would be lodged in local archives and so be kept for posterity. The presenter and Winnie discussed the sad lack of documentation in this respect, the conclusion being that efforts should be made to remedy the situation. I realised that Winnie was known to my wife and me since she and my wife had been pupils at Chatham Grammar School together. I had to agree that there was a scarcity of material available on this subject and since I had been evacuated along with many other children from the Medway Towns during the war I decided that I would provide a very brief account to add to her collection. Having penned a few pages which I sent on to her, I considered writing this account, so Winnie is to blame for the writing of what follows, my personal story.

Each memory from those dark days always prompted another, sometimes a trifle hazy. These memories are probably not in chronological order but I believe that generally they are. It has, however, caused me to return and to visit those places where I had to live more than fifty years ago. In so doing I have once again visited friends made all that time ago. Some I have always visited from time to time across the years but this time I have been able to check that my memory has not been playing tricks on me. I have

With Schoolcap, Label and Cardboard Box

confirmed many dates, names and locations whose accuracy was questionable and through these visits I have been able to renew more of the friendships that I had made during the war. From every contact that I made I have been encouraged to complete this missive. I hope therefore that this account of four formative years of my life, may give pleasure also to all those, who like me, were wrenched away from home to spend time in a different and sometimes unkind environment. Most of the photographs and illustrations that are included are more than fifty years old and in consequence the quality of reproduction may be poor. This is due to the condition of the originals.

I was born in Gillingham, Kent in 1927. My family arrangement was that I lived with my grandparents and I had done so from the age of six months. In consequence my grandparents were my parents as far as I was concerned and so I called them mum and dad. My grandfather was employed in the Dockyard at Chatham as a shipwright, my grandmother looked after the home and the rest of my family (mother, stepfather, stepbrother and stepsisters) lived locally at various addresses over the years but mostly in the Medway Towns. My education began at Richmond Road Infants School in Gillingham followed by attendance at Richmond Road Boys School where I passed the examination and won a scholarship to attend the Gillingham County School for Boys which was in Third Avenue.

For winning this scholarship my grandfather bought me a Hercules Roadster bicycle for the sum of three pounds twelve shillings and sixpence (three pounds sixty-two and a half pence in today's money). This represented a whole week's wage for him in 1938. This gift came as a very pleasant but unexpected surprise since he had not promised anything to persuade me to do well in this examination. Having collected this bicycle from Currys in the High Street I was pushing it home, no way was I going to scratch it on the way. On passing the side entrance to Gillingham Police Station in Jeffery Street, Detective Inspector Coe, who lived next door to us in Kingswood Road, detained me briefly but only to

Just before my tenth birthday.

present me with a brand new bell which he said had to be fitted on the handlebars before I rode it. It was the latest model bell at the time and had two domes that rotated when rung and sounded 'Ding Dong, Ding Dong, Ding Dong' in two tones. He obviously knew exactly when I would be going to collect the bicycle.

In the 1930s pastimes out of school hours were hopscotch, rolling hoops and whipping tops in the street, roller skating; all of these being safe since there were only two persons other than the doctor who owned motor cars in Kingswood Road. Other activities included playing with cigarette cards, or swapping them, marbles, tipsticks, conkers in the autumn, and sometimes annoying residents of the street by tying a string across the road to the knockers of opposite houses leaving a small amount of slack in the string, knocking on one door and running a short distance away to watch the fun. We hoped that when one door was opened the string would just lift the knocker of the opposite door and when the occupier found nobody at their door when they closed it the knocker on the other side would fall hard enough to cause that door to be opened and so on. This was usually done just before dark in the hope that the string would not be noticed. I must point out that most door knockers in those days were heavy iron ones unlike the lightweight ones so common nowadays. Indoors games included marbles, tiddlywinks, and I was lucky in that a bagatelle and a shove halfpenny board had been obtained for the family's amusement. Sometimes we played card games like *Snap* and *Beat Your Neighbour*, or board games such as *Ludo* and *Snakes and Ladders*.

I was expected to attend Sunday School each Sunday morning, mostly at the Salvation Army Citadel, but also for short periods at other establishments like the Church of the

With Schoolcap, Label and Cardboard Box

Seventh Day Adventists etc. depending upon which religious group was in my grandmother's favour at the time. Sunday School outings, certainly those that I remember organised by the Army, were to Sheerness mainly, where we were encouraged to compete in races on the grassed area close to the Railway Station and the Big Wheel of the nearby funfair. Usually the prize for the winner of any of these races was a few toffees. If the tide was in we were allowed to paddle our feet on the shingle beach. At Christmas a party was arranged either at a church hall or perhaps a cinema where we played simple games like musical chairs, spinning the plate, or pass the parcel and were fed sandwiches, fairy cakes and jelly and soft drinks. As we all left the hall at the end of the party we were presented with a brown paper bag which contained an apple, an orange, a few mixed nuts, a small bar of chocolate and a few toffees. At home on Christmas morning in my stocking I would find much the same selection of fruit, nuts and sweets, sometimes something fancy like a sugar mouse, and a board game or a jigsaw. I still recall finding a set of dominoes in my stocking one year.

In warmer weather, if my stepbrother and stepsisters were living locally (usually they were) I would visit them on a Saturday and perhaps take a picnic to the local woods, this being an occasion that we thoroughly enjoyed. If they were living in Walderslade, where they did for at least two years, I would walk both ways to visit them, a walk of almost three miles each way. On one of these trips into the Walderslade woods I was introduced to the stem of a creeper plant which the local lads called 'smoking cane'. A short length could be lit at one end and it could be smoked like a cigarette. Trying this experiment certainly brought tears to my eyes and accidentally inhaling brought on a violent fit of coughing.

With Schoolcap, Label and Cardboard Box

Holidays of any length were unheard of, my grandfather worked in the dockyard for five and a half days per week and his annual holiday was for just one week, that being the first full week in August when the dockyard was closed for work but open for 'Navy Week'. During this week visitors were allowed in the dockyard but only to one restricted area. Consequently, the family annual holiday was usually one day in the dockyard to see ships and displays and one day at a Kent coast resort like Sheerness, Herne Bay, or Margate, travel there being on board one of the pleasure steamers such as the *Medway Queen*.

Possibly we might go to Southend and visit the funfare called the Kursol. Otherwise there were trips to the Gillingham Strand, a sandy strip of beach on the River Medway. Sometimes from the causeway at the Strand we would take the penny ferry, a boat that carried about eight and rowed across the river to Upnor by a local fisherman. All simple pastimes but extremely popular with most of the population of the Medway Towns in the 1930s.

1938/39 was my first year at the Boy's County School and left me with few memories of note. Very quickly I learned to swim in the school's small pool, actually I was pushed into the water at the deep end after having been told that I would not be allowed out of the water until I had reached the shallow end. Fortunately, since the pool was small, I managed to hold my breath whilst frantically thrashing my way from one end to the other. No, I will not indulge in the pun! The sports day held at the end of the summer term of 1939 also comes to mind. I ran in the 440 yards race around the school field but did not do very well although I was not last. I competed in the high jump for my age group and won. There were just two of us competing at the final height and my opponent fell awkwardly at his attempt and damaged his wrist. I had managed to clear the bar which left me as the winner. I am not convinced that I could jump higher than Roy (that was his name) and the imminent evacuation caused us to lose touch. We were to meet again, however, about twenty years later when we both became trainee draughtsmen in Chatham Dockyard. I recall that one of the masters owned a small car, an Austin Seven I believe, and he would leave the school grounds and drive along Third Avenue no hands, whilst putting on his gloves. This he did every day!

The school's uniform consisted of a purple cap and blazer worn over grey trousers. The cap and blazer were adorned by a badge which included the White Horse of Kent and we were required to wear a white shirt with a purple tie with thin stripes on it set on the diagonal. Most boys hated the colour purple and would remove both cap and tie at the first opportunity and carry the blazer rather than wear it if the weather allowed. Usually this happened around the first corner away from school. As in most schools the teachers were given nicknames by the pupils and a few that I remember were 'Yorkshire' for Mr Dale the Headmaster, 'Spider' for Mr Webb, (he incidentally was both red haired and rather hirsute), 'Apple' for Mr Newton and of course 'Ding Dong' for Mr Bell.

During the tense days of August 1939 I was still enjoying the Summer holiday, not very aware of the political situation since I was only twelve, expecting to return to school to commence my second year there. However, due to the grave situation in Europe caused by the actions of Adolf Hitler, on Friday 1st September 1939, before the date that the school was due to open for the 1939/40 year, I, together with about two hundred other boys, arrived at the school wearing that

With Schoolcap, Label and Cardboard Box

purple schoolcap, blazer, tie, a label on which was written my name, form number and school name, a cardboard box containing a gas mask slung over one shoulder on a piece of string, a postcard to send home upon arrival at my new home, a small suitcase (which is still in my possession) containing a change of underclothes, night clothes, house shoes, spare socks, towel, toothbrush, knife fork and spoon, a mug, plate, handkerchiefs, a mac and some food, hopefully to last the day. This suitcase was destined to be the most

MEDWAY TOWNS EVACUATION SCHEME
Full Name of Child: *George Proger*
Home Address: *84 Kingswood Rd, Gillingham*
Name of School: *County Grammar, Gillingham*
School Number: *Form IIB*
Group Number:

The label tied to jacket lapel.

valuable possession during my years of evacuation, for with the exception of my short stay at my first billet of the war, space for another body together with clothes and a few possessions in the other billets proved to be scarce. I found that I was forced to store my clean clothes and any of my personal items in that case, generally under the bed. It could be said that I lived out of that case plus maybe a hanger or two on a hook on the bedroom door. That case measured just 20 by 13 by 7 inches, and was bought specially for the occasion at Woolworth's in Gillingham.

With Schoolcap, Label and Cardboard Box

The suitcase. It still has two carriage labels stuck to it. One for ten old pence and the other for eight old pence – railway charges.

Shepherded by members of the school staff we made our way to Gillingham Railway Station where in the meantime many parents had assembled. We were to be evacuated and we knew not where! Most of us considered that this journey away from home was to be a sort of holiday and a lot of misgivings about leaving home were balanced by thoughts that at least we knew many of those going away with us and it was going to be one big adventure. For many of us it was just that – an adventure. For me it was to last until I was old enough to commence work!

After a relatively short journey, in distance but not in time, the train arrived in Sandwich in Kent where we were met by local dignitaries and townspeople who had offered to host evacuees. In the Town Hall, next to the Market Square, we were served with light refreshments before a start was made to sort out who went where. Difficulties were encountered when it was discovered that there were only boys in the party whereas many of the townspeople had intended that they would take girls only to their homes and not boys. Eventually they were prevailed upon to take us and our hosts took us away to their homes, mostly in ones or twos. A fellow evacuee named Norman and I were finally adopted by a very attractive lady who reluctantly agreed to take us. We were certainly in the last four to be allocated, and I am sure that initially we were taken 'on trial'. We both climbed into the back of a large motor car, owned it was said by an ex-army officer, our belongings were deposited beside us and we were transported to what appeared to us to be a large house, situated quite close to St. George's Golf Course. We discovered that this lady was a film star named Judy Gunn and that there were several other film stars, Mary McGuire was one, living in the nearby houses. The house was named Sandown Lodge, it still bears that name. Judy's married surname was Hue-Williams and her husband was a member of the River Police, Thames Division, and since he was based in London he spent only occasional weekends at home. In the garage was a large American car but he used an Austin Seven with a fabric roof to drive to and fro.

Norman and I were very fortunate to be billeted there since we were cared for by the lady of the house together with a cook and a young maid. There was a very young baby, a Pekingese dog and a black cat completed the list of residents.

Two incidents took place the following day, Saturday. Firstly, dinner was served in the evening, not at midday as was usual in our own homes, and after the meal we were introduced to coffee served in tiny bone china cups, very strong, black and syrupy with a thin slice of lemon. What

TOWN CLERK'S OFFICE,
GUILDHALL, ROCHESTER.

TOWN CLERK'S OFFICE,
TOWN HALL, CHATHAM.

TOWN CLERK'S OFFICE,
MUNICIPAL BUILDINGS,
GILLINGHAM.

24th March, 1939.

EVACUATION.

DEAR SIR or MADAM,

The Corporations, at the request of the Government, are now preparing plans for the voluntary evacuation of school children in the event of a national emergency. This does not mean that there is immediate danger. The object of the Government is to make plans in time of peace, so that, if an emergency were to arise, all concerned would know the part they ought to play.

The purpose of this circular is to assist you to decide whether or not you wish your children to be evacuated in case of emergency.

The Scheme is quite optional. Parents are at liberty to decide the matter for themselves. It must, however, be remembered that if you decide beforehand not to have your children evacuated it will probably not be possible to consider a last minute application on the outbreak of, or during, hostilities. Transport arrangements are being made only for voluntary evacuees under this scheme.

The plan now being prepared by the Government provides for the children to be sent in the charge of their teachers or other responsible adult helpers to places where they will be more widely scattered. Children from the Medway Towns would probably be transferred to areas in various parts of Kent. It will be appreciated that in War time no place would be absolutely safe—one can only speak in terms of *comparative* safety—but the Medway Towns, with the Dockyard, Military and Naval Establishments would undoubtedly prove a formidable target for aircraft attack which would seriously endanger the lives of those who live in the district.

Many people would have to stick to their posts and take their chances. Possibly you come under this heading. If so, it is for you to decide whether you would not prefer to entrust your children to their teachers to take them away to some safer place.

It is proposed to board the children out in homes in small towns and villages. They would be supervised day and night by the teachers and other helpers, and arrangements are being made by the Government for medical attention where necessary.

One of the main concerns of the Government in organising this dispersal of the children from the crowded towns is that they should not lose their education. Obviously it would not be possible to send them all to schools such as those we have in the Medway Towns. Some of them might even have to be taught in Mission Halls, Cinemas, empty houses, etc., but everything possible would be done to keep them busy and happy, and one is quite sure that the country people would do everything possible for them.

So far as possible, all the children in one family would be kept together. The scheme provides that, on assembly for evacuation, the younger children of the family may if you desire accompany their oldest brother or sister, from the school which he or she attends.

It would not be possible before the children leave home for the parents to be told precisely where they are going, but arrangements will be made for the parents to be informed by post within a day or two of arrival of the whereabouts of the children.

No expense on the part of the parents, either in respect of transport or maintenance, will be involved.

At the foot of this circular will be found a list of articles of clothing, etc., that the children will be advised to take with them when evacuated.

It is impossible in this statement to cover the whole scheme that has been carefully worked out. The Head Teachers are well acquainted with the details of the scheme and if you desire further advice before coming to a decision you are invited to call at the school which your child or children attend and see the Head Teacher, who will assist you in every possible way.

If you decide to allow your children to take part in the scheme will you please complete one form for each of your children and return it to the Head Teacher of the School which the child attends.

Yours faithfully,

J. L. PERCIVAL,
Town Clerk, Rochester.

EDWARD B. LEE,
Town Clerk, Chatham.

ROBERT BOOTH,
Town Clerk, Gillingham.

List of articles of clothing, etc., which the children will be advised to take with them on evacuation.

HAND LUGGAGE.
  The child's gas mask.
  A change of underclothing.
  Night clothes.
  House shoes or plimsolls.
  Spare stockings or socks.
  A toothbrush.
  Knife, fork and spoon.
  Mug and plate.
  Comb.
  Towel and handkerchiefs.
  A warm coat or mackintosh if possible.

FOOD FOR JOURNEY.
  Sufficient food for one day.
  It will be unwise to allow water or other drinks to be carried, because of the risk of broken bottles.
  Apples or oranges are most suitable.

Any parcels that the child may carry should be labelled with his or her name, home address and school.

The letter that the local councils sent to parents during 1939.

Assembling outside Gillingham Station in Balmoral Road. Photo: Kent Messenger.

About to board the train at Gillingham Station platform. Photo: Kent Messenger.

With Schoolcap, Label and Cardboard Box

Sandown Lodge in 1997. George Prager collection.

luxury! Surprisingly very thirst quenching! Secondly, when the maid cleared the dishes at the end of the meal and prepared to wash them she dropped a milk bottle onto the red tiled kitchen floor but instead of the bottle shattering into pieces it bounced off the floor and she succeeded in catching it. The look of relief on her face I can still remember. I feel sure that she thought that she might have been sacked otherwise. Norman and I usually were required to take our meals in the kitchen but we were allowed into the lounge in the evenings provided that we were well behaved.

War was declared on Sunday 3rd September 1939. I clearly remember that the whole household was assembled in the lounge on that Sunday morning at 11 a.m. to hear Prime Minister Neville Chamberlain, in sombre tones, broadcast to the nation on the wireless. The actual declaration of war was at about 11.15 a.m. An air raid warning siren was sounded

With Schoolcap, Label and Cardboard Box

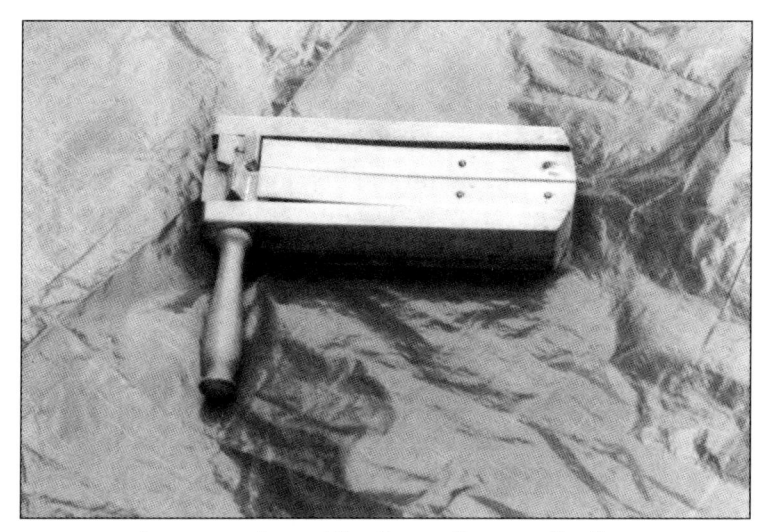

A gas warning rattle. George Prager collection.

immediately and the all clear about two minutes later. The warning was either just a reminder of the sound or a subtle signal that we were at war. The sounding of rattles in the street was to be a signal of a gas attack.

School attendance commenced the very next day at Sir Roger Manwood's and a few days later I heard that one of the older boys had spent only one night at his allocated billet before being moved. Apparently upon waking in his bed on that very first morning he discovered to his dismay that he was absolutely smothered in flea bites, and on reporting it to one of the masters was instantly moved to another address.

Whilst researching material to confirm the accuracy of some of my recollections I spoke on the telephone to an associate with a shared interest in local history, a person that I rub shoulders with week by week so to speak, and discovered that he had attended the Gillingham County

With Schoolcap, Label and Cardboard Box

School for boys as did I and that he had been evacuated on that same day to Sandwich. During our conversation he remarked that he would always remember his first night there and for good reason. I asked him why that was and he replied, 'When I woke up on the first morning I found that I was completely covered in flea bites and so was moved at once to a new billet.' It certainly is a small world!

In brief articles that I have read in newspapers and magazines a comment common to many has been that many evacuees were infested with either fleas or lice when they arrived at their new homes. It was true also that 'clean' evacuees were placed in homes that were infested that way.

Quite a few homes did not have a bathroom, or even a bath! This was overcome by boys billeted in such conditions being taken along to the public baths each Tuesday evening.

We were expected to attend Sir Roger Manwood's School but the lack of space there could not accommodate pupils from both schools. There was a problem also that air raid shelter provision for such numbers was inadequate. This resulted in shift working in the classrooms, and the local Methodist and Congregational church halls, large rooms in private houses such as the Ramparts, the Salvation Army, a Scout Hut, and ironically a shop that had been the Fascist Headquarters, all being pressed into service as temporary accommodation. This accommodation was spread over a distance of about two miles and sometimes caused waits between lessons whilst members of staff moved from place to place leaving the boys where they were. Whenever there was a lack of space for lessons we were taken for walks around the area and this was usual also on free half days. Priority was given to those boys in the fifth and sixth forms of both schools who had important exams in the current year, the sixth forms of both schools being merged and working almost full time. Visits to the cattle market in the town, the Town Hall, the Butts, the Toll Bridge, and churches in places like Worth and Woodnesborough all come to mind. Walking beside streams, fishing for sticklebacks, visiting the beach in Sandwich Bay via the golf course were all tried and mostly enjoyed. I recall picking blackberries, especially those through the chain link fence of a garden near to my billet. These berries were larger and juicier than those along the hedgerows because they were being cultivated purposely by the owner of the garden. This was a form of scrumping I suppose!

Norman and I became friends with Gordon the son of the steward of St. George's Golf Course and there we learned the rudiments of the game. We borrowed two or three clubs from one of the members and were allowed to play on a practice hole of about two hundred yards which had a tee and a green of sorts at both ends. We spent quite a few happy hours playing on this hole forwards and backwards and became quite expert at hitting the ball but not so expert in achieving the right direction. I suppose it could rightly be called a nineteenth hole, but not the bar in the clubhouse!

Catering for the members of the club was excellent since food was not yet rationed. Quite often there would be food surplus to the needs of members in the club dining-room and occasionally we would be allowed to sample some of the dishes. It was here that I tasted fresh salmon salads for the first time and often there were mouth watering 'tasters'. Gordon was a favourite of one of the waitresses there so we three boys were 'treated' frequently. Gordon had developed a distinct liking for hard boiled eggs and whenever some had been prepared for inclusion in the salad dishes, he would try to help himself to one whilst no one was looking. This he did one lunch time and because he had to pass by one of the waitresses on his way out of the dining room he popped it into his mouth whole, hoping that she would not notice. In this he was successful, but unfortunately Norman and I were running up the stairs that led to the dining room just as Gordon emerged through the doorway to come down. Norman was leading the way, head down and consequently his head met Gordon's stomach. 'Ooops!' the egg was forcibly expelled from his mouth and flew through the air towards me. My reflexes were good and I made the perfect catch so saving his favourite snack!

One day another boy and I decided that we would walk all the way to Ramsgate, about seven miles, but I cannot remember if we ever got there. I can recall however that we became decidedly thirsty after several miles and knocked at the door of a wooden bungalow and asked politely of the elderly lady who answered our knock, could we please each have a glass of water to drink? 'Certainly,' said this lady, but when she brought them to the door we found that the water was quite brown in colour and tasted so earthy that we could not drink it!

Food rationing began on 8th January 1940 and the allowances were:-

    bacon 4 ounces

    butter 4 ounces

    sugar 12 ounces per person per week.

Meat was rationed from March 1940 but this was by price and not by weight – this meant that you could have more if you took a cheap cut.

In July of that year cooking fats, cheese, jam and tea (2 ounces) went on ration.

With Schoolcap, Label and Cardboard Box

Eggs became limited to one per week, and after a short period they were limited to one per fortnight.

Milk, cereals, biscuits, canned fruit and fish all became restricted in some way, but children were allowed milk, cod liver oil and orange juice: these by a daily quantity.

Large tins of National dried milk and dried egg were soon on restricted availability as substitutes for the fresh.

Bread was not rationed but was sometimes in short supply, usually due to erratic supplies of flour to the bakeries.

(Bread did go on ration for a while but not until after the war had ended.) At the announcement of the rationing of sugar I solemnly stated that henceforth I would drink tea without it. At home all of my family drank tea with sugar and so tea served up for me always contained sugar as a matter of course, assuming that I preferred it that way. Put to the test I discovered that I preferred it without, for now I could taste the tea. Sugar had been hiding the taste. I have drunk tea without sugar ever since, now one sip of sweet tea is awful!

There was an allowance paid to those who had taken in evacuees and this amounted to just ten shillings and sixpence for the first and eight shillings and sixpence for each extra. (Fifty-two and a half and forty-two and a half pence respectively at today's values.) Since most growing boys had a hearty appetite this was an amount that probably fell short of the cost to their hosts. Parents could make a donation towards that cost and this had to be made to the County Council's Accountant. Whether this contribution was voluntary or compulsory I am not sure. (This was contrary to the statement in the Local Council's letter stating there would be no charge:- see page 10 last para.)

During the winter of 1939/40 there was a fairly heavy fall of snow which lingered on the ground for just over a week.

With Schoolcap, Label and Cardboard Box

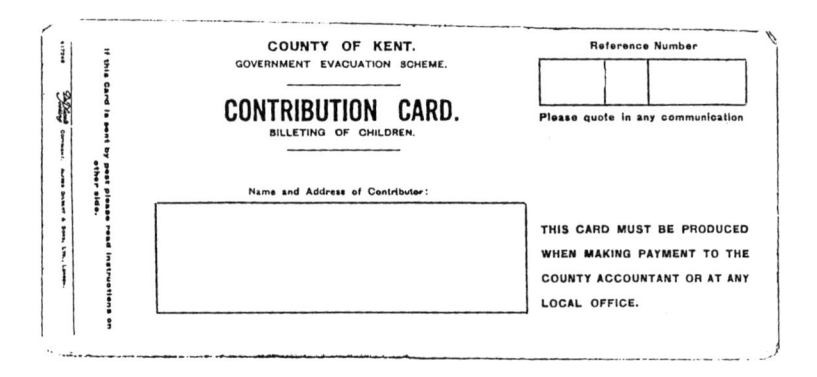

```
COUNTY OF KENT.
GOVERNMENT EVACUATION SCHEME.

CONTRIBUTION CARD.
BILLETING OF CHILDREN.

Reference Number

Please quote in any communication

Name and Address of Contributor:

THIS CARD MUST BE PRODUCED
WHEN MAKING PAYMENT TO THE
COUNTY ACCOUNTANT OR AT ANY
LOCAL OFFICE.
```

During this snowfall we were still required to play rugby football on the school field and were sent on cross-country runs in singlet and shorts around the edge of the field and along nearby roads and footpaths. Over the weekend a school chum and I set off early to the beach of Sandwich Bay, crossing the golf course as a short cut. On the way across the course I disappeared into one of the bunkers, almost up to my neck. Undeterred, having extricated myself much to the amusement of my chum, we continued on our way. As I was already soaked, once we reached the water's edge I decided that I would take a dip in the briny. As we were the only ones in the bay I stripped off, and tried to persuade my pal to join me. He considered me to be either mad or foolish, perhaps both: in I went, stark naked, and when the water reached my knees threw myself in! Brrr! Was that water cold? Gasping for breath with the shock that I experienced, I came out faster than I had gone in. Running backwards and forwards along the beach in an effort to warm up and trying to get dressed again in wet clothes was a real struggle and so uncomfortable. Slowly, by running around and with the help of a breeze blowing from on shore, my clothes dried on my body and I experienced that very warm 'after glow' that you get after your flesh has been in contact with snow. Just like that feeling you get after having thrown snowballs with bare hands. I felt warm for the rest of the day, but my clothes were a sorry sight and of course they had to be washed to remove the salt.

The road from Sandwich to St. George's Golf Course passed over a stream, the rather narrow bridge being almost directly outside Sandown Lodge and one of the younger members of the Golf Club owned a green Bentley sports car, one with a large brown leather strap securing the bonnet. He was a 'devil may care' type and often drove over the bridge at breakneck speed. Two or three times a week we would hear the growl of the car's engine at night as he sped away from the club, usually awakening the household! On one occasion I was at the clubhouse when he arrived in that magnificent car and parked it at speed by skidding it sideways on the gravel which flew in all directions, much to the annoyance of the groundsman.

In early March 1940 I made a sightseeing trip into Deal and, having some money left from that given to me when I left home, I decided to purchase a camera. I spotted one in a chemist's shop window priced at five shillings (twenty-five pence now). I believe the chemist was a branch of Timothy White's and appropriately the camera model was called 'Crown'. I also bought three rolls of film for it. Soon film became rather hard to obtain due of course to the restrictions imposed as a result of the war. This camera started a fascination with photography that grew over the years and has remained with me right up to the present day. Back at Sandown Lodge I used the first roll of film on the first sunny weekend in April by taking pictures of Judy Gunn with her baby, with the Pekingese dog, and then persuaded her to take pictures of me.

The masters in those days, like those of today, each had their own methods of dealing with pupils who did not pay them the required attention during lessons. If a pupil was obviously not concentrating on the subject, it was very likely that he would be reminded of the fact by a piece of chalk being thrown accurately in his direction, the target usually being the culprit's ear. Sometimes it might be a blackboard rubber thrown to land nearby. One of our masters was fond of using the culprit's own wooden ruler by picking it up from the desk and rapping him smartly over the knuckles. The particular occasion that comes to mind was when this happened to a boy sitting next to me. We were all sitting around a long table since there were no desks available in this substitute classroom. The master picked up the boy's ruler and administered the rap over the knuckles but unfortunately this ruler had a metal strip set in its edge which cut into the boy's fingers and the next moment there seemed to be blood everywhere! The injuries were promptly attended to and to my knowledge that incident banished such a method of chastisement and it was never applied again!

Since no air raids had occurred at Sandwich or Gillingham up to the end of April 1940 many of the boys had returned to their homes either at the wish of their parents or because they were very unhappy at being away from home. Some parents thought it quite safe to bring their children home because there was no bombing experienced in those early days. There were various reasons for bringing them home. Most children had not been away from home before and in many cases brothers and sisters were separated and they were experiencing a completely new way of life, perhaps lack of

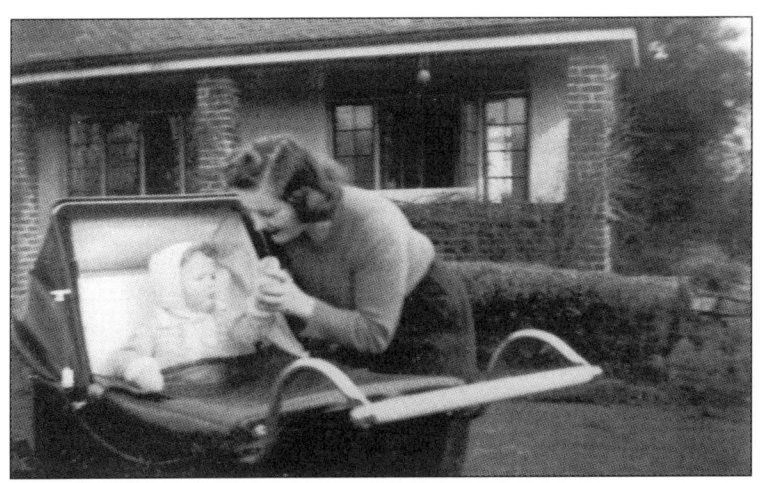

Judy Gunn with her baby at Sandown Lodge 1940.
George Prager collection.

George Prager at Sandown Lodge. George Prager collection.

noise, shops and the way of life appropriate to the town or city. Some of the country folk had strange ideas of how the children lived at their homes, such that manners were missing and that they ate with fingers. Parents maybe found that they could not afford to visit their children because of the distances involved, and the foster parents did not want the town parents to come if it meant they had to stay overnight or longer and they would have to be fed. Later, after at least two more evacuations, children became worried about their parents' safety, especially when the bombing became serious. All of these reasons were responsible for evacuees returning home irrespective of the possible consequences. This period was later known as the 'phoney war' and with changes in homes caused by young men either volunteering or being pressed into the services there was much movement of people, either in moving to 'safer areas' or to be with members of the family who had to move for one reason or another for their job.

Norman and I had to leave Sandown Lodge because of a change in the domestic circumstances of Mr and Mrs Hue-Williams who had to leave for the London area in which he was stationed and we were moved to the Golf Course Clubhouse with Gordon's parents. Gordon's father joined the RAF and with the situation across the English Channel deteriorating such that the German Forces were fast approaching the coast of France and the evacuation of our troops becoming imminent, those of us still in Sandwich were put on a train that was to transport us to Cardiff in South Wales. So Norman and I spent just two weeks at the clubhouse, two weeks with such wonderful meals that we felt that we could not do better staying at a first class hotel, before we boarded that train with about forty boys and four masters.

With Schoolcap, Label and Cardboard Box

The train journey took most of the day travelling along the south coast. I feel sure that like me most of the boys considered it to be a great adventure. I for one had never travelled so far on a train before. We stopped for a short while at one station for simple refreshment and there at another platform was a train crowded with battle weary soldiers. They were being given cups of tea, cigarettes etc. Afterwards I realised that they were men who had been brought home from France.

By this time many people had dispensed with their gas masks, either forgetting them or finding that carrying that cardboard box on a piece of string over the shoulder was just a nuisance. The masks were usually kept near to hand in the house and the cardboard box or the leatherette case that some had invested in became convenient containers in which to carry lunchtime sandwiches.

Our stay in Whitchurch, Cardiff, was of very short duration and all that I can remember was a visit to Llandaff Cathedral. We had moved from Sandwich during the last week in May and on 2nd June the main school in Gillingham suffered a second evacuation, this time to Rhymney, a village at the head of the Rhymney Valley, one of the Welsh coal mining valleys. On 8th June those of us at Cardiff were uprooted once again to join the rest of the school. Most of the available billets that were close to the school which we were to attend had been taken by the main influx of the week before, so we late arrivals were billeted farther away than most. My new address was at Pen-y-Dre, which loosely translated means 'top of the town', and was at the northern end of Rhymney.

I had not come into contact with Welsh people before so I was not prepared for their accents nor their sing song style of

At 20 Pen-y-Dre 1940. Door of No. 21 in background.
George Prager collection.

With Schoolcap, Label and Cardboard Box

Nos. 20 & 21 Pen-y-Dre 1998. George Prager collection.

speech which mixed English words with a selection of Welsh ones. Everyone was very friendly, particularly adults, and most would recognise us as evacuees and call across the road to us when passing, but sometimes the words they used were unintelligible. One evening a gentleman neighbour called out to me whilst passing on the other side of the road and, apparently pointing skywards said, 'North Star.' That is what I thought he had said. I looked up into the sky in the direction I thought he had pointed and could see nothing of a star through the clouds. Puzzled, I mentioned the incident to another neighbour nearby and he laughed and said 'He was only waving to you and wishing you goodnight. The Welsh for goodnight being Nos Da.'

I cannot remember either Mr or Mrs Knight using more than an odd word in Welsh so we did not need to use any to communicate but a few boys learned some basic Welsh so that at least we could pass the time of day with those natives that spoke to us so. these were

Bore da	Good morning
P'nawn da	Good afternoon
Nos da	Good night
Diolch	Thanks
Diolch yn fawr	Thank you very much
Dim diolch	No thank you
Cymru	Wales

We just had to learn to say Llanfairpwllgwngyllgogerychwyrndrobwillantysiliogogogoch.

This was a real challenge and after persevering for several days we managed it. I am not surprised that it gets shortened to Llanfair p g nowadays. The school that we were to attend was called The Lawn and was situated almost at the southern end of Rhymney. Again accommodating the pupils of two

The Workmen's Institute Rhymney. Marion Evans collection.

Boys from Gillingham County School assembled in the quadrangle at the Lawn School soon after arrival in Rhymney. Photo: Mary Pinkney.

schools in the premises intended for one was impossible, so at first each worked a half day shift in the school until extra accommodation was found. The Workmen's Institute cum library (this was next door to the school), the Masonic Hall and the Social Centre were very quickly pressed into service, but until they could be made available, games, mountain walks, table tennis, cricket, rugby – what else in Wales? Some Welsh boys expressed surprise that an English Grammar School actually taught their boys to play the game. There were also trips to the next door valley at Tredegar for swimming at the pool. We Gillingham boys quickly discovered that the basement of the Workmen's Institute contained a number of full size snooker tables. Happily it was soon arranged that these tables were made available for us to use at so much per half hour's play. A coin was put into a slot meter and this switched on the light over the table for a pre-determined period. In the corner of the room was a small counter at which we could buy soft drinks. The hall was occupied by us whenever we could escape from lessons and we all learned to play both snooker and billiards in double quick time. To hire a table we needed money so running errands became very popular.

The early days were fraught with danger whenever we dared to venture south to Pontlottyn since the local Celts always seemed to have a sixth sense that we were invading their territory and would welcome us with a well aimed volley of stones, pieces of slate or coal, even pieces of housebrick! It was obvious that we were not welcome! It is a surprise to me, on reflection, that none of us ever suffered serious injury, just bruises or minor cuts and abrasions. After suffering these attacks for some weeks we decided that we must retaliate by returning their fire. Most of us played

With Schoolcap, Label and Cardboard Box

cricket, or had done so back at home, and one or two of us were fairly accurate bowlers, so, one day we armed ourselves with missiles of various forms and headed for Pontlottyn. As soon as our adversaries appeared we let fly with some accuracy, catching the Celts by surprise. Discovering that we Londoners, as they liked to call us, could give as well as we could take, a truce was called and an end to the conflict agreed. This resulted in friendly relationships being formed between the groups, some of them lasting to the present day.

The houses in Pen-y-Dre were typical of council houses built in many areas of the country in the 1930s and my new hosts were Mr Knight who was a guard on the railway and Mrs Knight who kept house. A fellow schoolboy whose name escapes me, and myself, were the other residents, although there was a son Leslie, but he was away from home working most of the time and I met him only once. About half of Pen-y-Dre had houses on only one side with open mountainside on the other and the other half had houses on both sides. About two hundred yards away on the mountainside and near Susannah's Row a spring rose out of the ground, and at some time a metal pipe had been driven into this spot so that the issuing water was guided clear of the ground. This allowed containers like buckets etc. to be placed under the end and filled easily. The water from this pipe was always icy cold, crystal clear, safe to drink and constantly flowing. From this spot a well worn path led over the mountain to the Tredegar Valley and this became a favourite walk for me during the summer and autumn months of 1940.

On several occasions whilst taking that path to Tredegar I stopped at the 'armchair' to take in the view. The armchair was a natural depression in the mountainside in the shape of such a chair and about four of us could sit side by side in it.

With Schoolcap, Label and Cardboard Box

Close to this spot there was often a card school, a group of local men playing cards for money, this of course was contrary to the laws of the day. These schools were always in a saucer shaped dip in the ground and might gamble for hours. Always there were two younger men or teenagers sitting close by as lookouts so that a warning could be passed if a policeman should appear on the scene. Upon such a warning being given the cards would disappear immediately into one pocket and the money would go likewise into another man's pocket and the school would nonchalantly disperse, usually leaving the two lookouts talking casually. Unless the police actually saw the gambling no action could be taken. Frequently, soon after such a visit when the policeman was out of sight, the school would return and continue from where they had stopped.

It was possible also to walk most of the length of Rhymney north to south with the the backs of houses on one side of the path and the mountainside on the other, and this became the favoured route to and from school each day.

Exploring Rhymney and the surrounding area during the summer months of 1940 was fascinating and full of adventure. We found the old iron works on one side of the road to Rhymney Bridge and the River Rhymney on the other. At the site of the old iron works we discovered the remains of an iron furnace, an old and rusty iron ore truck still standing on a short section of railway, and pieces of pig iron, obviously either discarded or perhaps spilled when the molten iron had been poured close by. In the rock pools of the river we were able to fish but again I can only remember finding and sometimes catching sticklebacks. At Rhymney Bridge Railway Station it was possible to stand in three counties at once. The official boundaries of Glamorganshire,

With Schoolcap, Label and Cardboard Box

Monmouthshire and Brecknockshire met on the station platform so that with just one foot placed precisely you could stand in all three. From just north of here it was possible to see all the way to the Brecon Beacons. We made many excursions to the Beacons area. On several occasions we walked all the way to Merthyr Tydfil via Dowlais Top, and although we were too young to frequent them, there seemed to be a public house every few yards from Dowlais Top all the way down to the centre of Merthyr Tydfil. I have been informed since that there were 142 pubs on that stretch of road at that time. Near the bottom of the hill on the way down from Dowlais there was an arch built from large blocks of coal. This was built over a side road turning off to the left. This was a source of wonder to us since the only coal that we had seen before was in pieces of a size suitable for putting on the fire. Sadly this arch has been removed, but I feel that it should have remained there or have been re-erected somewhere locally as a fitting memorial to all of the coal miners that worked in the area for so many years.

At home, in the days pre-war, it was usual to see animals like cattle, horses and sheep constrained behind fences or hedges. Of course we were used to seeing tradesmen's horses on the street, like bakers, brewers and milkmen, delivering their wares. In the valleys, however, only cattle were so constrained and they seemed to be very few. Sheep and ponies could be seen almost anywhere, on the mountains, in fields and almost every day on the roads, very often in the towns and villages. If a garden gate was left open, either a sheep or a pony would arrive and be cropping away at any green shoots that could be found. They were all adept at opening a gate or finding a way through a small gap.

At breakfast one morning, at Pen-y-Dre, unbeknown to me

The Coal Arch. Photo courtesy of Merthyr Tydfil Central Library.

The river at Rhymney. Opposite the old furnace.
George Prager collection.

2

She has had a bad cold, but is quite well again, and is taking some Malt. I have in the house, I bought it for mrs Knight but he did not like it, so George is taking it. We will soon have Christmas, with us, it wont seem like it, for a good many, will mr Coleman be working. I think most people everywhere will be working. This war is looking bad, it will be nice to see it all over, and everything back to normal again but I am afraid its going to be a long time before that happens, and we must all live in hopes of better times to come, no more to say now so will close. From Yours Sincerely
mrs Knight

Part of a letter to my grandmother from Mrs Knight, Nov. 1940. This I found with papers of my grandfather's after he died in 1951.

there was a shortage of bread, just enough for one slice per person, and although my co-evacuee was aware of this he failed to inform me, so I helped myself to a second slice to satisfy a healthy appetite. This resulted in me receiving an ear bashing on the theme of my being greedy and lacking consideration for others. When I asked my colleague why he had not told me of the situation he just shrugged his shoulders and walked away.

Another morning, trying to be helpful, I picked up some of the dishes from the table after breakfast intending to take them into the kitchen ready to be washed. Opening the door to the kitchen I was confronted with the lady of the house having a wash at the kitchen sink stripped to the waist! Of course I got an eyeful! When I was forcibly admonished for daring to open the door I could only apologise both profusely and blushingly, whilst wondering why she had not used the bathroom like the rest of us!

Although Mr and Mrs Knight were very kind and treated the two of us with every consideration I feel that for some reason they could not let us get very close to them. We were kept at a distance. An example of this was that a letter sent home to my grandmother by Mrs Knight was signed Mrs Knight. I never did discover either Mr or Mrs Knight's christian name.

The daughter in the house next door, Peggy Humphries, was about the same age as we two evacuees and when her birthday arrived her mother kindly invited us both to a party, together with several other teenagers living nearby. Although some food was rationed by this time Mrs Humphries managed to lay on a generous spread. There was tea, lemonade, both fizzy and still, sandwiches, home made buns, biscuits, sweets, chocolate, jelly, custard and blancmange, with some tinned fruit. I think she must have raided the reserves and maybe the families involved pooled some of their supplies. It was the best party that I had been to!

It was from the youngsters of Pen-y-Dre that I learned to play a game that was unknown to me before. Locally it was called 'five stones' and was played with five small pebbles, or frequently with five small pieces of coal about the size of dice used with most board games. I believe that this game is more commonly called 'Jacks', but has names peculiar to the area in the country in which it is played.

During the winter of 1940/41 there was a heavy snowfall and I decided to photograph sunlit snowscapes. The glare from the snow was so bright it was painful to my eyes and after about half an hour I developed a splitting headache and felt decidedly sick. I took three or four shots and then made my way back to the house as quickly as possible. I sat quietly in an armchair for about two hours before feeling better. Mrs Knight insisted on my being checked over by the local doctor and he said he thought that I had suffered a mild form of snow blindness but had acted sensibly by returning and resting.

During that same winter, in late November 1940, a British aircraft crashed on the mountain above Pen-y-Dre. This occurred during the night at about 2.30 a.m. and the noise of the crash woke most of the residents in the vicinity. There was much conjecture as to exactly what had happened but most of us were of the opinion that the pilot had attempted to land on the mountainside. Unfortunately the plane had been too low coming in over the top where it lost its undercarriage and then slid down the mountain on its fuselage. This was borne out by the fact that the wheels and legs were found left behind nearer the top. Individuals from

With Schoolcap, Label and Cardboard Box

the neighbourhood were very soon on the scene, and the first 'official' to arrive was a special police constable from Rhymney Police Station who was nearby at the moment of the crash. This policeman was to become very well known to me later on during my stay in the valley. The crew were taken to the local cottage hospital and their injuries were treated by the doctor on duty there that night, Iain Evans. I believe that one crew member died but the rest survived. Quite a few small souvenirs disappeared from the crashed aircraft, mostly small fragments of aluminium, but the RAF salvage team arrived very quickly, soon after dawn, recovered the plane and cleaned the area leaving nothing but the furrow in the ground. This incident was the talk of the town for some time with the inhabitants of Pen-y-Dre recounting how lucky they were that the plane had stopped short of crashing into houses on the street. The plane had bombs aboard! The bombs had been removed and were exploded on the mountainside whilst we teenagers were at school. Such excitement. Especially to young teenagers!

Attempting to confirm my recollections of this incident I appealed through the local newspapers for recollections from local people in the Rhymney area. I received more than a dozen replies, letters and telephone calls, some being in remarkable detail, but only three agreed with my recollection generally, but not completely. The rest gave details that varied of the plane's make, different locations for the site of the crash, differences in the number of men in the crew, and differences in the names of the policemen first on the scene. As a result I have written my version of the event in the belief that it is correct.

One of my classmates obtained some laxative chocolate sold as 'Ex-Lax' and for some fun shared it around piece by

With Schoolcap, Label and Cardboard Box

piece with several of us after having carefully scraped the name off each piece. The following day there were several absentees from school, me included. We had suffered the result of eating that laxative but we thought that it was from some other cause, such as eating too many sour apples or food that was slightly 'off'. The amused culprit was taken to task however once we discovered he was to blame. We de-bagged him in the boy's toilet and made him suffer that indignity for about an hour as revenge. I hate to think what the result might have been if he had given us more than one piece of that chocolate each.

In the early spring of 1941, on a warm sunny day, my co-evacuee and I managed to borrow a bicycle each for an excursion. We decided that we would ride southward, possibly to Cardiff, but we did not realise just how far that was. Neither of us had a watch, nor did we have any idea of how far we might be capable of riding in a day. Since we did not ride regularly we were sadly out of practice. Anyhow, off we went at a leisurely pace, not a care in the world, enjoying the warm sunshine and a wonderful sense of freedom, there being next to no traffic on the roads. The few sandwiches and a bottle of fizzy lemonade that we had taken with us we consumed whilst sitting on a grassy bank at the side of the road after about three hours on our saddles. We resumed our ride and eventually arrived in Caerphilly, this being only about half of our intended journey. By this time we were feeling rather tired and suddenly became concerned about the time. We soon realised that it was early evening and that we had no lights on the bicycles, nor did we have more than a few coppers in our pockets. There was no telephone at our billet, there were very few telephones in ordinary houses at that time, a telephone being a luxury for only the rich or

Signalman, Guard Ernie Knight, Driver Jack Patten, Fireman George Brown. Photo: Cyril Patten

With Schoolcap, Label and Cardboard Box

famous or perhaps a necessity for the larger business. In any case we did not know anyone in Rhymney that might possess one so we had no way of passing a message to say where we were. We had not had the sense to tell anyone where we intended to go. We thought of trying to persuade a bus driver to take us back to Rhymney on his bus with a promise that we would arrange payment of our fares on arrival, but then what would happen to the bicycles. We would not be allowed to take them on the bus and we could not leave them behind since they did not belong to us, and anyway they probably would not be safe left behind. What a quandary! Quite by chance we discovered that we were not far from the railway station and it occurred to us that the railway could be our salvation. We had remembered that Mr Knight was a guard on the railway and we could put bicycles on a train. So we made our way to the station and fortunately found a sympathetic porter to whom we recounted our sorry tale. By this time it was almost dark. When the next train for Rhymney arrived this kindly porter escorted us to the guard's van at the rear of the train and explained our predicament to the guard. To our great surprise and relief the guard was Mr Knight! All he said was, 'Put those bikes in the van, get yourselves in and stay put.' He then walked along the platform and we assumed that he went to obtain tickets for us. Were we pleased to see Mr Knight? Certainly we were! We were not so pleased though with the lecture we both received all the way home! We were warned also that we would have to repay the money for the fares from whatever pocket money we had or could earn by running errands. However he relented later and said, 'Just let that be a lesson to you both. Do not go off without saying where you intend to go!'

At the end of the spring term of 1941 a number of boys

With Schoolcap, Label and Cardboard Box

returned to Gillingham, some of them miserable and dispirited. This created vacancies in billets near the school and being at some distance from the school in Pen-y-Dre I was selected as one who could be moved. Maybe also because Mr Knight had to work odd hours on the railway, our being in the house was disruptive to his routine, we two evacuees were moved. My co-evacuee went to another billet and my move was to a small house hardly more than one hundred yards from The Lawn and in the High Street. Two boys had moved out and gone home to Gillingham. They were Des Lacey and the other boy whose surname was Hope, his christian name escapes me. Previously, together with the house next door it had been a butcher's shop. It consisted of two rooms up and two rooms down with the stairs leading up from the downstairs back room. The front room down had the front door opening straight onto the pavement outside, but the man of the house, a special constable, the policeman who was the first 'official' on the scene of the plane crash I mentioned earlier, had built a wooden partition to create a passageway from the front door to the back room thereby separating the front door from the front room. Built onto the back room was what could be described as a narrow conservatory which served as a kitchen cum skullery. Outside the back door from this kitchen a flight of stone slabs set on brickwork served as access to an apology of a garden and an open area under the house, the property being built on a hill. It was as if the back wall of the house had been built on stilts. Part of this area under the house had been partitioned off to screen an outside W.C. There was a hard floor and the rest of this space was devoted to storing such items as buckets, brooms, shovels and here too was the zinc coated tin bath which was usually hanging on a nail in the wall. In the

With Schoolcap, Label and Cardboard Box

depths of winter visiting the loo was a case of putting on the winter woollens first or being brave but rapid! The garden was a small dirt area with a fence dividing it from next door. In the garden was a small wooden shed that served as a workshop and contained the woodworking tools belonging to the man of the house. A similar sized garden was at the rear of next door but access to the lane at the bottom of the gardens was only through the one gate in ours. The back boundary of the garden next door was the rear wall of one of two cottages in that lane which led out to Tre York Street. Tre York Street led from the High Street downhill past the Workmen's Institute, The Lawn School to the railway station. Close to the station were some tennis courts, a building used by the Council as offices, one part being the Headquarters for Civil Defence and a few yards away was the Cottage Hospital. At the end of the lane at the bottom of the garden and leading into Tre York Street were two cottages with their rear entrances facing along the lane.

Soon after I had settled at this new billet I chanced to go out of the back gate and into the lane early one windy morning. Standing in the lane and smoking a cigarette was an attractive blonde lady who lived in the nearest of these two cottages at the end of the lane. She was waiting for her Pekingese dog that was exercising itself in the lane and doing what dogs need to do. (It was surprising just how many ladies owned Pekingese dogs as pets in those days – the fashion of the time I suppose!) To my surprise I noticed that this blonde lady was dressed only in a long flowing pink silk dressing-gown and because it was a windy day her gown had parted from just below her belted waist. She was displaying one bare leg together with a dark triangle of pubic hair! Completely unconcerned or possibly unaware of this disclosure although

Tom Pritchard, Special Constable. Photo: Douglas Pritchard.

Tom and Jennie Pritchard in back garden.
Photo: Douglas Pritchard.

With Schoolcap, Label and Cardboard Box

she was aware of my presence, she called her dog and calmly walked indoors! I was just fourteen and this was my first experience of such a sight. The first question however that popped into my head was 'Why did that lady have fair hair on her head but black hair down below in that most intimate place?' Young teenagers in the 1940s were not so knowledgeable as those of today but I soon learned about the results obtained by the use of a bottle of peroxide and other methods of changing hair colour.

At this house in the High Street lived Tom and Jennie Pritchard and their son Douglas who was about five years my junior. Tom was the policeman I have already mentioned and the Police Station was just two hundred yards away along the street. Tom always maintained that it took a rogue to catch a rogue, and I suspect that many policemen today also subscribe to that statement. He and I had a discussion at the dinner table one day about the benefits of being as observant as possible. Certainly it was necessary to be so as a policeman he said and he made much of how useful it could be to me in my studies. I took these comments seriously and thought that I would be clever a few days later when I spotted him in the distance just leaving the police station and about to start on his afternoon patrol. I immediately stepped into a shop doorway so that I was out of his sight and waited there patiently as he walked towards me on the other side of the road. As he got closer I moved quietly into the shop and watched him pass by. My intention was to challenge him as to which of the two of us was the more observant that day, so I waited until he came home from duty at 10 p.m. that night. Imagine my disbelief and dismay when at the moment he walked into the house he said, 'What were you doing skulking in Fishlock's doorway this afternoon?' Obviously he had spotted me first and then deliberately looked the other way as he walked past. Was I deflated? Definitely!

Fishlock's was a small general shop on the corner of Cross Street and the first thing to be seen on entering the shop usually was an enormous cat, invariably asleep on the end of the counter. I cannot remember its name but it must have weighed twenty pounds or more and all it seemed to do was sleep.

The custom of the Welsh people at this end of Rhymney was that they operated an 'ever open door' attitude to all of their relations, friends and neighbours and this was rather difficult to get used to at first. Although friendly to all of the neighbours, both in my previous billet and at home in Gillingham, an ever open door policy was certainly not acceptable at either address and would certainly not be countenanced by my grandparents. Front doors were never freely open to all and sundry. A front door key was only ever allowed to a special friend and that was only in the event of an emergency. In Rhymney High Street however it was an accepted routine. All were allowed to walk into the house without knocking, for the front and back doors were never locked except at night or when the house was unoccupied. They would say 'Hello' as they stepped into the back room, the front room seldom being used, and sit down at the table or in any convenient chair, just as if they owned the place. The ever boiling kettle on the range immediately went into use to brew tea, seemingly endless pots of it. Instantly they would engage those members of the household present in discussion and debate, usually at the top of their voices. After a good session they would just stand up and walk out of the back door! If you forgot to slip the latch so that the door was fastened it could result in an embarrassing situation of receiving visitors unannounced whilst taking a bath. Since there was no bathroom the zinc coated tin bath was set on the floor in front of the range, cold water being brought from the conservatory/kitchen and hot from that large ever boiling kettle on the range. My first experience of having a bath in front of an unexpected audience was very disconcerting! I must say though that having a bath in front of the fire in the range was the height of luxury! It did mean that blushes could be denied and being flushed was due to the hot water and hot fire. Presumably the adults bathed after we young ones were asleep in bed, or whilst we were at school during the day. With Tom on shift work as is normal in the police force this would have been convenient and with the doors locked no doubt! I discovered that it was quite common in miner's houses however for the miner to wash off all the coal dust in a bath like that irrespective of who might be present.

This back room, in which we all ate, drank, bathed and spent doing homework and other leisure activities was lit after dark with gas. The gas lamp hung from the ceiling directly over the centre of the table, itself in the centre of the room. Having drawn the blackout curtain over the window, a chain dangling from the gas fitting was pulled downwards slowly until the gas could be heard hissing gently and the gas was then ignited using a lighted match, taper or twist of burning paper. The gas flow had to be adjusted until the mantle glowed brightly. To extinguish the light a chain had to be pulled on the other side of the fitting. Because the room was blacked out before the gas was lit this had to be done using a torch or most times by judgement. The mantle was protected by a clear glass shade about the size of a two pound jam jar. Maybe you, the reader of these words, may not have seen a two pound jam jar. I must say that I have not seen one for many years. If the gas was turned on in a hurry and the chain was pulled down further than usual the sudden heat generated by the flame could make the glass shatter. If this should happen and a replacement glass was either not available spare in the house or not in stock at the hardware shop a two pound jam jar could be adapted to fit. This was normally done by tying a piece of string around the jar about a quarter of an inch from the bottom, the jar stood on its open end, the string soaked in paraffin or a similar inflammable liquid, lit and as soon as the flame had subsided the jar was plunged into cold water. Most times this resulted in the bottom of the jar being removed cleanly leaving no sharp edge. A mantle could not be substituted however but these were generally available from Joseph's shop which was next door to the Scala cinema, almost opposite the police station.

Clothes rationing started on 2nd June 1941 and the restrictions were based on an allowance of one complete outfit per year. For shirts, trousers and underclothes many boys existed with a wardrobe that consisted of one each being worn and two, possibly three for underclothes, sets in the wash and in the wardrobe.

The clothing coupon allowance was 48 per year. A lady's good quality woollen frock cost £3 and 11 coupons. Ladies' overalls cost eleven shillings and nine pence and a boiler suit fifteen shillings.

Generally our morale was high. Listening to the wireless was commonplace, always hoping for good news such as success in one of the battle areas. Very often bad news was censored or made light of. Lord Haw Haw with his claims of Nazi successes, mostly seriously exaggerated, provided endless amusement. Very few took his pronouncements seriously. On

With Schoolcap, Label and Cardboard Box

Thursday evenings Tommy Handley's programme ITMA (It's That Man Again) was so popular that possibly the whole nation came to a standstill to listen.

Most newspapers printed cartoons using war events as subjects of fun. *The Daily Mirror*'s cartoon strip every day was most popular and its subject 'Jane' became one of the nation's pin-ups. Jane was always depicted in some embarrassing situation, generally being short of clothing. For most lads of my age the cartoon page was usually the first to be looked at, always eager to see how many clothes she had managed to discard! Comics were also available, such as *Beano, Dandy, Hotspur* and the like and often the characters in those comics were used to promote wartime slogans.

Just a short distance along the High Street was a grocer's shop owned by Abel Evans and in order that I might earn some pocket money he was persuaded to employ me to help in the shop and deliver orders to customers. This was done on Friday after school and on Saturdays until about 4 p.m. if required. These times were during term time and occasionally on other days during holidays like Christmas when customers orders were somewhat larger, depending of course on whether extras were available.

I became quite proficient in weighing up commodities such as flour, sugar, tea, rice, soda crystals etc. All of these items and others like butter, margarine, bacon and biscuits were supplied to the shop in bulk and had to be made up according to the customer's allowance (ration). Items like tea, sugar, flour and rice were weighed and packaged in cones of blue paper of the appropriate size. These cones were made by rolling a square of paper around one hand with the other and the cone so formed was twisted at the bottom so that it was secure, then the contents were poured into the top of the

1941

FAST ASLEEP!— I CAN SLIP OUT AND SEE IF TOMBS HAS FALLEN INTO MY TRAP!
POOR DEAR JANE CAN'T GET AWAY WHILE SNOOP IS ON GUARD OUTSIDE....
?
DOWN, FRITZ!— WHY—WHAT—? —SOMETHING FISHY'S AFOOT!!!
THE WINDOW'S STILL MY BEST MEANS OF EXIT— WHILE SNOOP IS AT THE DOOR!
NOW WHY DID LOLA LEAVE THE BEDROOM?—SHE'S UP TO NO GOOD I'LL BE BOUND!— WHAT'S HER GAME?
WHY—THERE SHE GOES!— A MIDNIGHT RAMBLE AT THIS TIME OF YEAR!!?
?
GOOD HEAVENS! —THERE GOES THE SIREN!— AND I CAN HEAR A PLANE OVERHEAD!!!
NOW WHERE DID LOLA GO?
GOODNESS!— SOMEONE'S FLASHING A LIGHT IN THE WOODS! —SIGNALLING TO THAT PLANE!
HELP!
IT'S ALL RIGHT, MISS JANE!— IT'S ONLY ME!
TOMBS!— HOW YOU SCARED ME!— WHAT ON EARTH ARE YOU DOING HERE?
WHY, YOU TOLD ME TO MEET YOU AT THE HOLLOW TREE AT MIDNIGHT, MISS JANE!
NOT ME, TOMBS!— THIS LOOKS MORE AND MORE LIKE LOLA'S WORK...
YOU'D BETTER SCRAM BEFORE YOU'RE SEEN!
I'LL GO BACK THE WAY I CAME, MISS!

1941

NO SIGN OF LOLA AT THE HOLLOW TREE–SO FAR....
THAT BLINKIN' NAZI AIN'T SHOWN UP YET!
IT LOOKS AS IF TOMBS IS GOING TO FUNK IT–CURSE HIM!
BUR-RUMPH!

A BOMB MUST HAVE FALLEN IN THE GROUNDS!
NO WONDER–WITH ALL THOSE LIGHTS FLASHING!
HELP, COLONEL!–JANE GOT AWAY–SHE'S BEEN SIGNALLING THAT NAZI BOMBER WITH A TORCH!

FEB
1

TAKE CARE, LIEUTENANT–SHE'S PRETENDING TO FAINT!
SO WE'VE CAUGHT YOU OUT AGAIN!–GOOD WORK, LOLA!
WELL–!–I'M DASHED IF I CAN UNDERSTAND ALL THIS!–IF JANE'S A SPY I'D BETTER RETIRE FROM INTELLIGENCE!!!
I'LL CARRY HER IN!–HOW LIGHT AND FRAGILE SHE IS!–IF ONLY SHE WEREN'T–A TRAITOR–!

WHERE AM I?–WHAT'S HAPPENED?
YOU'RE A PRISONER IN HUSH-HUSH HOUSE–AND LUCKY TO BE ALIVE!
I–I THINK I'D LIKE A BATH!
WHAT–AGAIN?–THEN YOU'LL HAVE IT UNDER AN ARMED GUARD–YOU'RE A SLIPPERY CUSTOMER!
ALWAYS IN HOT WATER–AREN'T YOU, DARLING?

1941

-ER—TELL ME. WHO IS YOUR WAITRESS?—I'M SURE I'VE SEEN HER BEFORE SOMEWHERE...
YOU MEAN LISA?- A PRETTY GIRL- YES?-ALMOST AS PRETTY AS MADAM!- I TELL YOU HOW I GOT HER...
BUT BEFORE ANTON CAN PROCEED...
....THE SAILS OF THE MILL BEGIN TO REVOLVE IN THE WIND AND....
CREAK!
HELP!
WHOOSH!
GOODNESS!— WHAT A WIND!
HEAVENS!—IT HAS STARTED THE MILL!- THE SAILS SHOULD BE LOCKED!!!
WHOOSH!
THAT GIRL MUST HAVE TAKEN THE BRAKE OFF!- IT WILL SHAKE THE OLD PLACE DOWN AT THIS RATE!— I MUST STOP IT!
WHAT'S THIS?— THAT SLIP OF PAPER LOLA GAVE JOSS!—
IT'S ONLY THE BILL— BUT— SOMETHING'S WRITTEN ON IT....
WHOOSH!
YES—IT'S JUST THE BILL—BUT HERE'S A SCRAWLED MESSAGE!—
Achtung!- Jane is here!— A WARNING!
AND HERE COMES JOSS!— I MUST AVOID HIM!
WHOOSH!
LOLA WENT INTO THE MILL— TO START THE SAILS, NO DOUBT, AND CREATE A DIVERSION!
I'LL FOLLOW HER!
IT LOOKS— PUFF!—AS IF THOSE TWO ARE HAND IN GLOVE, FRITZ!
HIST!—ANTON AND THE WAITRESS ARE UP THERE, FRITZ!
HOW DARE YOU MEDDLE WITH THE BRAKE, LISA!— THIS WIND WILL SHAKE THE OLD MILL DOWN!
I AM SORRY, MR. ANTON!— IT VOS AN ACCIDENT!— I PLAY WIZ IT, SEE!
GO BACK TO THE TEA GARDEN AT ONCE—I MUST STOP THE FANTAIL!
GOSH! SHE MUSTN'T SEE ME HERE!— I KNOW—
—I'LL GO DOWN ON THE SAIL!

'Jane' cartoon strips courtesy Mirror Group Newspapers.

With Schoolcap, Label and Cardboard Box

YOU CAN HELP BRITAIN BY COLLECTING WASTE-PAPER

Desperate Dan of the Beano comic and the waste paper saving poster.

cone which was folded over and tucked in. The contents had to be safe and not leak out. There was a lot of laughter at my first attempts to create a safe package, but practice made perfect and this task was quickly mastered. Judging how large a piece of cheese should be to be of a certain weight, how much butter, salted or unsalted, margarine, rashers of bacon or ham off the machine to exact weight were all tasks I was required to master. Sometimes several hours were spent in weighing up just sugar into half pound, one pound and two pound cones, or tea starting at quarter pounds and rice or flour in the same way. When making up orders the items for each one were gathered together in a pile on the counter, checked by Abel and placed in a separate cardboard box or large paper bag if only a small quantity, the order being checked against the bill which was then placed with the package ready for loading in Abel's car, unless the customer's address was nearby. These I normally delivered on foot. With the orders packed securely on the back seat of the car Abel and I would start a round trip to Pontlottyn, Abertysswg, Tredegar, Rhymney Bridge and back to Rhymney. Abel's car was an Austin Ruby Saloon of about 1935, chocolate brown in colour with black wings and running boards. Car deliveries were made on Friday evening and Saturday morning with Abel driving and I would assist with the actual delivery,

With Schoolcap, Label and Cardboard Box

opening gates on farms, and finding the order from the piles on the back seat. The remaining local orders were for me to deal with on Saturday afternoon.

Petrol was rationed of course, but because Abel had customers at a distance from the shop he was allowed extra to make such deliveries. Private owners had been made to lay up their vehicles for the duration unless they had genuine needs. Merchants like coalmen, bakers and milkmen needed vans for their deliveries but there were many that used a horse and cart. Taxi drivers were allowed fuel but were supposed to operate only within a five mile radius of their business premises.

After a few weeks Abel noticed that I paid particular attention to how he drove the car. He started to give me a running commentary on what he was doing and why. This led to my moving the gear lever into whichever gear he required whilst he drove. One day, on arrival at the garage after deliveries were completed he suggested that I might attempt to put the car in the garage. We changed seats and with trepidation and very slowly I managed to do so without mishap. After doing this several times with him sitting beside me without me damaging either car or garage it became a routine that I would unlock the garage, drive the car out into the lane where the garage was located, relock the doors and wait for Abel. This was whilst he finished his breakfast. The reverse procedure was carried out when deliveries were complete. Whenever we were on private land after that I would turn the car ready to depart to the next call and Abel would make the delivery and receive due payment. My grandfather was reluctant to believe that I was driving a car at the tender age of fourteen! Driving tests were not required at this time but of course I was still too young to be allowed to

With Schoolcap, Label and Cardboard Box

An Austin Ruby car like Abel's except it had four doors.

drive on the roads. I did however drive on the road for about a mile and a half with the connivance of Abel's brother-in-law who stood in for him one day when he was not well. The road on which I drove that day has now been replaced by the Head of the Valleys Road in the Princetown area. That was probably the most exciting experience for me during my very early teens. Abel never knew of that escapade.

One Saturday morning, after having made the final delivery, which was in Tredegar, Abel stopped the car on the way back on the mountain road to give a lift to a lady customer who was waiting for a bus. Having stopped Abel asked me to get into the back seat so that the lady could sit in the front. The back seat was completely covered with empty boxes and cartons so I opened the rear door and started to rearrange the boxes to make room for myself. To do this I stood with my feet just under the side of the car which was standing on a downward slope at that moment and Abel must have been holding the car still with his foot on the brake. I did not notice the car move slowly forward until my left foot was trapped under the tyre of the rear wheel.

With Schoolcap, Label and Cardboard Box

Immediately I made my predicament known to Abel he put the gears into reverse but as he let out the clutch the car moved just a little forward onto my foot before it moved backwards to release me. The extra weight on my foot caused me considerable pain just for an instant but fortunately no lasting injury. Examination of my foot on return to the shop revealed that the tip of my big toenail had been forced through the leather upper and the toe was red, slightly swollen and throbbing. A bruise developed and the next day it covered all of the toe and had spread part of the way along my instep. I limped for a couple of days and the bruise took a long time to fade.

As well as the commodities that I have mentioned I recall that biscuits also were supplied to the shop in bulk, in tins each of about a twelve inch cube. Their contents were transferred to air tight tins arrayed along the front of the counter, each with a hinged lid in which was set a glass panel so that the customer could see the contents. The container nearest to the shop door always contained broken biscuits and any pieces of biscuit discovered during weighing up of the contents of any of the other containers were transferred to it. These broken biscuits were very popular and the quantity allowed to each customer had to be restricted. As the war progressed tinned fruit was often in very short supply so whenever fresh fruit was in season and if there was a good quantity available some was always set aside for preserving, usually by bottling. At the shop a consignment of tinned fruit arrived one day and upon opening the case we found that it contained 14lb tins of Canadian produce, apples. In order to give our customers fair shares we appealed for clean jam jars and the next Friday evening was spent opening the tins and transferring the apple into the jars. They were covered with a piece of greaseproof paper and secured with string. Quite a few apple pies were enjoyed I am sure.

It might be of interest for me to note here that whenever ingredients could be scraped together for pies and pastries there were some quite imaginative concoctions arrived at. One that became popular was to use boiled and mashed parsnips with a fruit flavouring added as a filling for a fruit pie. If the filling did not look the part then a food colouring would be added as well for disguise. Even after the war a well known manufacturer used parsnip as an addition to real fruit to make the fruit go farther. I have sampled mashed parsnips this way with banana essence added and it is difficult to tell it from actual mashed banana. If meat pies were obtainable then they were of minced meat with lots of gristle. Whalemeat and horsemeat were tried in some parts of the country but was not too popular. Mainstays of dried milk, dried egg, and spam (still available even today), together with the humble potato were predominant in most households and with root vegetables like carrots, turnips, swedes and the like it was amazing the variety of meals that were created.

Potatoes and vegetables of all kinds were grown wherever suitable plots of land could be dug, whatever the size. DIG FOR VICTORY was a slogan that appeared all over the country and probably was one of the most effective of the war years.

As well as the incident when my toe was trapped by the car wheel there were two other occasions when I escaped serious injury. Firstly I was with a group of boys exploring an area of run-down buildings, such places have a strange fascination for boys even today, and we all climbed onto a wall that was about fourteen feet high. We sat side by side on top of this wall and decided to drop to the ground one by one. This we

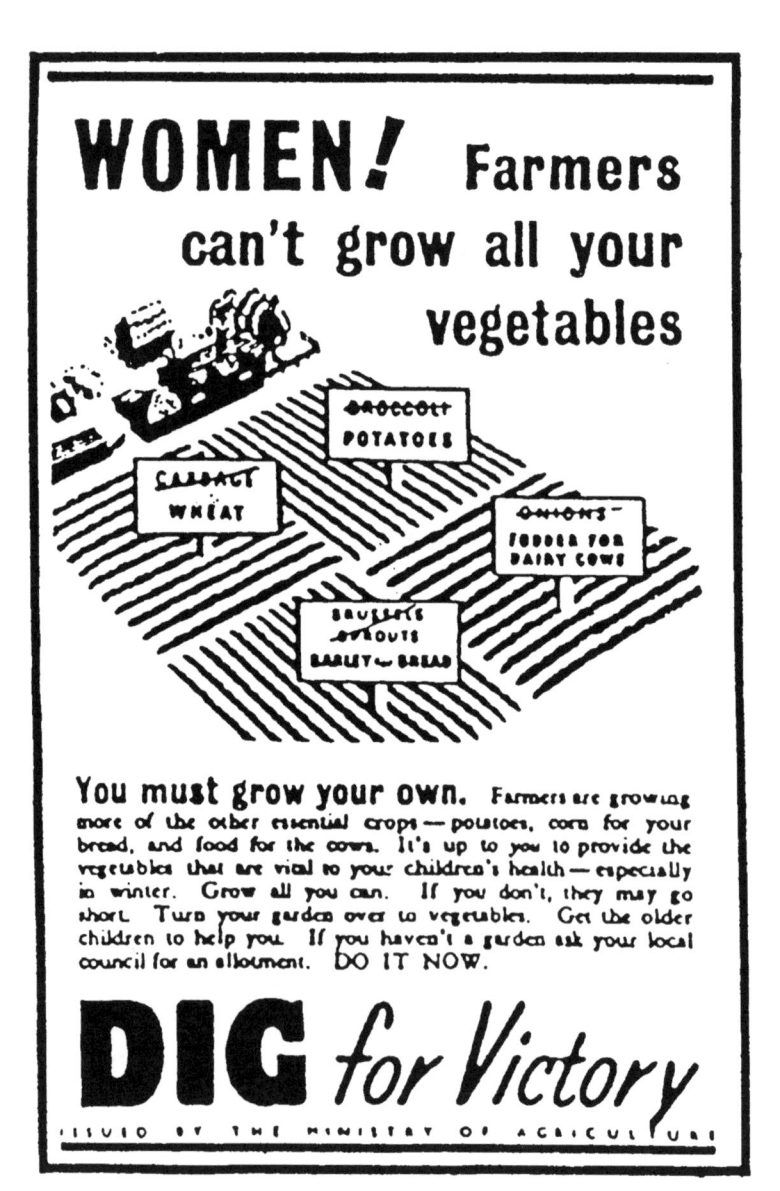

A typical 'Dig for Victory' poster.

With Schoolcap, Label and Cardboard Box

did, three before me, then I landed safely as well, but before I could move out of the way for the next boy to drop, he dislodged a loose brick which struck me a glancing blow on the left temple. As with all head wounds this caused me to shed what appeared to be an excessive amount of blood. With some consternation the boys almost carried me to the nearby Cottage Hospital. The wound was only superficial and with a small amount of hair shaved away, a clean up and a sticking plaster all was well. However I think that I rather revelled at playing the unconcerned warrior.

The other occasion was when three of us had met at one boy's house. To the side of his house was a small walled-in piece of ground the entrance to which was a wooden gate about the size of an average front garden gate to a terraced house. This gate was formed from two side uprights and two rails, one top, one bottom, with a diagonal cross joining the corners. We were at this gate discussing what we might do and where we might do it and I had climbed onto the gate and was sitting on the top rail with my feet tucked into the vee formed by the cross. A decision arrived at the other two boys moved away from the gate but as I attempted to get down my feet were wedged in the vee. Consequently I fell head first against the wall that was about four feet away opposite. I had the presence of mind to turn my head sideways and ended up striking the left side of my head (again) against a rusty nail protruding from the wall.

This pierced the skin and also made a small hole in my skull just above my ear. Fortune smiled on me once again since the mother of the boy who lived in the house was a nurse at the Cottage Hospital. She cleaned and probed the wound and pronounced that I would live in her opinion but insisted that I went to the hospital for it to be checked.

With Schoolcap, Label and Cardboard Box

This I did and I was given an injection in my rear. The embarrassment in having to drop my trousers was worse than the accident! I still have that small scar over my left ear.

For a short while I helped on a milk round in return for a small sum. This involved meeting early each Saturday morning the milkman who used a small open backed truck about the size of a present day milk float. With another boy helping as well we would start the round in Abertysswg and deliver all the way to the centre of Rhymney. After nine o'clock we would deliver the bottles and collect the amount required in payment and pass it to the milkman. In Rhymney we parted from him after having received our payment and he would return to Abertysswg to collect monies from the rest of his customers. The daily milk at our house in the High Street however was delivered by a milkman with a horse and cart, (it was either Mr Lance or Mr Moseley). The milk was carried in churns on the cart and was dispensed from the churn by dipping a long handled galvanised steel measure of the appropriate size into it and pouring it from the measure into a proffered jug. This milk was much creamier than that delivered in bottles. Frequently the stop at our house was the time for the milkman to enjoy a cup of tea in the house whilst the elderly horse contentedly munched hay from a nosebag. A thank you deposited by the horse onto the road immediately disappeared into someone's bucket and eventually found its way onto a garden.

Sunday was chapel day. It was also 'monkey parade' day. There were churches in the area, but most of those residents that attended Sunday services were chapel-goers. After attending chapel on Sunday morning a great number of the young people would 'parade' in their Sunday best clothes by walking and talking up and down the main street, up and down, up and down: in Rhymney this was of course the High Street and Church Street. This would continue for all of the day if the weather was kind, and in the summer months it continued until dusk, (with double summer time, that was with the clocks two hours forward, dusk could be 11 p.m.), with a lull perhaps during evening service. Much of the 'courting' was carried out this way or going to the cinema during the week, hoping of course to sit in the back row. Public houses were closed on Sundays as were most of the shops. I believe that one or two clubs were allowed to open on a Sunday and I remember that one enterprising shop owner, Mr Gambarini, opened in the evening in the winter when he served hot drinks, most of which were made from blackcurrant cordial and 'Vimto'.

School holidays were spent roaming the local countryside, mostly with Douglas or boys from school. We would take a snack if possible, our favourite being Welshcakes, provided that Jennie had been able to bake some. These were flat, sweet, scone-like cakes laden with fruit (sultanas being the best) which were baked on the range on a flat iron plate (a griddle or bakestone), this being placed on the open fire of the range. In summer we would supplement these snacks by picking and eating Wimberries that grew wild on grassy parts of the mountains. I am told that Wimberries are called Bilberries, Blueberries, Wortleberries, Blaeberries, and Huckleberries as well, depending whereabouts in the country you live. Even in the valleys I have seen them called Windberries, Whinberries and Winberries. The fruit is deep purple in colour when ripe but has a bloom on it as do black grapes. This makes them very difficult to spot in the grass to an inexperienced eye but like blackberries they stain your fingers to a bright purple colour. They make the most delicious filling for a pie so we would try to take enough home for that purpose. Even today (1998) I consider them to be a mouth-watering delicacy with a taste difficult to equal using any other fruit! Welshcakes and Wimberry Pie are two pleasures still remembered from those days now more than fifty years ago.

During our excursions on the mountains we discovered the 'Bent Iron' situated on top of the mountain to the east of the Rhymney Valley. This was an iron girder stuck in the ground, originally upright, but bent and twisted to a rather strange shape. We often set out with the iron as a target since if we tried to take the most direct route to it the climb was most difficult, and this was a challenge. To do this we had to climb up on loose scree and then for every step taken upwards the scree might move us two or three downwards. when the top was reached the view over the valley was rewarding. Taking the direct route down was completed in a very short time, the scree usually taking charge and often we would travel several hundred yards on our backsides! None of us knew at that time how the iron had become bent but in later years I have been assured that it became so when scouts built and lit a huge bonfire around it to celebrate the Silver Jubilee of King George V and Queen Mary in 1935. As a result of these jaunts on loose scree (mostly slag heaps of small pieces of slate and coal) many boys ended up with small fragments embedded in their flesh, usually knees. Over years these fragments might move about but still remain in flesh or maybe come to the surface to be removed easily. I believe that I still have two small pieces in one of my knees but they have never caused any pain or problem.

There had been a slow and gradual return of boys to Gillingham after the Battle of Britain so after the end of the summer term of 1941 the majority of those still at Rhymney returned with the staff to their premises in Kent leaving behind just one master with about thirty boys, the intention being to stay on for just one more year. A letter from the Ministry of Health in June had exhorted parents with children still evacuated to leave them where they were. My grandmother had died and my grandfather preferred that I should stay, partly persuaded by that letter I presume, but also because he would have had difficulty in looking after me whilst working long hours in Chatham Dockyard.

I did not know until I carried out some research into local newspaper files in 1997 that my grandmother had in fact taken her own life in April 1941: it was reported that she had become very miserable because I was so far away from home and that the rest of the family had left the locality to live and work in Scotland. The added worry of being on her own during the day with the possibility of bombs falling was just too much. So I was to stay and with the other boys that remained was integrated with the pupils of the Lawn School. This absorption was such that three Gillingham boys won first prize for singing in Welsh at the School Eistedfodd.

I believe it was about September that there was some rejoicing by Rhymney folk in the return from internment of Albino Dallanegra who owned a shop in Upper High Street. He had been interned when Mussolini declared war on this country in June 1940. He was renowned for his delicious home made ice-cream and for hot meat pies. (At least he was for the evacuees.) I am not aware that others of the same nationality by birth were treated in the same way. Mr Gambarini, who had the sweet shop and Mr Cordani, who sold fish and chips are two that come to mind.

Just before Christmas of 1941 a snooker competition was

A MESSAGE FROM THE MINISTER OF HEALTH
TO PARENTS WHO HAVE EVACUATED THEIR CHILDREN

MINISTRY OF HEALTH
WHITEHALL, S.W.1

You are among the many fathers and mothers who wisely took advantage of the Government's scheme to send their children to the country. I am sorry to learn that some parents are now bringing their children back.

I am writing to ask you not to do this. This is not easy, for family life has always been the strength and pride of Britain. But I feel it my duty to remind you that to bring children back to the congested towns is to put them in danger of death or that is perhaps worst, maiming for life.

You will have noticed that the enemy is changing his tactics.

He is now concentrating heavier air raids on one or two towns at a time, leaving others alone for the moment.

Nobody knows which town he will attack next so don't be lulled into a false sense of security if your home district has been having a quieter time lately.

Remember that in April over 600 children under sixteen were killed and over 500 seriously injured in our raids.

Do keep your children where they are, in the reception areas.

Don't bring them back even for a little while. This is your duty to the children themselves, to the A.R.P. Services in your home town, to those who are working so hard for them in the country, and to the nation.

I know that at times you feel lonely without your children and, believe me, I sympathise with you.

But you know as well as I do that it is far better to feel lonely now than to take a risk you may regret for the rest of your life.

Please read this message as the sincere words of a friend both to you and to the little ones.

Yours sincerely,

Ernest Brown.

June 1941

Will you share a small burden with your neighbour?

This little girl is billeted with Mrs. Brown. She is one of 400,000 children now safely in the country. She came last September with a label nearly as big as herself, a fugitive from a danger zone.

There were difficulties at first. It took her quite a while to pick up the ways of country folk. But when she settled in, Mrs. Brown grew quite fond of her. Mrs. Brown will miss her when she goes. But go she must. Mrs. Brown's circumstances have changed. Just as the circumstances of many other foster-parents are changing. They need someone to take over their small burdens.

These children must not go back to the cities. There may be raids at any moment. New billeting volunteers are badly needed. Will you enrol your name for this splendid national service? You may be asked to take a child now, or your name may be kept against the time when raids make a second evacuation necessary.

The Minister of Health, who has been entrusted by the Government with the conduct of evacuation, asks you urgently to join the Roll of those who are willing to receive children. Please apply to your local Council.

A Health Ministry poster of 1940.

GILLINGHAM WOMAN'S SUICIDE

Depressed Since Daughter Went Away

It was stated at an inquest at the Medway Technical College, Gillingham, on Tuesday, on Mrs. Annie Coleman, aged 56, of 84, Kingswood-road, Gillingham, who was found dead in the kitchen of her house, where she had hanged herself, that she had been suffering with her nerves and had recently complained of feeling very depressed.

Her husband, William Edward Coleman, a shipwright, said that just after Christmas their married daughter left home to join her husband in Scotland, and the deceased had appeared worried and been depressed since then, but she had never threatened to take her own life.

Charles Thomas Weekes, labourer, who stated that he had been staying with the Colemans for about thirteen years, said that when Mrs. Coleman's daughter went away it seemed to "break her up."

Mrs. Mildred Laura Garrett, of 96, Kingswood-road, Gillingham, said that just after 2 p.m. last Saturday she went round to see Mrs. Coleman. She found the back door open and called to her, and on getting no reply she walked into the kitchen. She then saw Mrs. Coleman, who appeared to be standing in a doorway leading into the living-room. She had her hands up to her throat, and witness went up to her and felt her face, and it was very cold. Witness then went for assistance.

In reply to questions by the Coroner (Mr. T. B. Bishop), witness agreed that Mrs. Coleman had sometimes seemed very depressed. She used to say "funny things" and was very restless. She liked company and did not like being by herself.

Police-constable W. E. Gumb handed the Coroner a blue scarf, which he said Mrs. Coleman had used to hang herself with from the top corner of a door in the kitchen. Nearby he found a chair.

Dr. Cecil Houet gave evidence as to examining deceased and said that death was caused by asphyxia due to hanging.

Summing-up, the Coroner said: "It seems quite clear from the evidence that this unfortunate woman was suffering very much from depression, and which was presumably due to the fact that her daughter had gone away from Gillingham to live. She had, I suppose, a temporary brainstorm and took her own life, and obviously the verdict must be one of suicide whilst the balance of her mind was disturbed."

In recording the verdict, the Coroner expressed his deep sympathy to Mr. Coleman in his tragic bereavement.

organised to raise funds for the British Red Cross. This was open to all comers and was to be held at the Workman's Institute where as I have previously mentioned there were numerous tables. It was a knockout competition of just a single frame per pairing. Just for fun I entered and much to my surprise, although I had to play much older competitors, I reached the semi-final. I cannot remember how many frames I played but I recall that I had a bye in one round when my opponent failed to appear. I lost the semi-final but did not disgrace myself against a recognised good player. So much for misspent hours after school!

I am afraid that I, like many other evacuees, did not write letters to my home as often as I should have done. Always there were things to do that were much more exciting than putting pen to paper. Very often my hosts would perform this task in my stead, informing those at home in Gillingham of any news regarding my health, progress at school, behaviour and activities. Many years later, after my grandfather was deceased, I discovered that the school had, without fail, sent termly reports to my home and they had been filed safely away by my grandfather amongst his important papers. Having a somewhat art bias in the subjects that I studied at school and having both a liking and an aptitude then for the subject, I often spent time on winter evenings making Christmas and Birthday cards, painting them in watercolours and sending them home. Often too, I would draw something on a postcard, such as a plane, Spitfire or Hurricane of course, or maybe a ship that was in the news, perhaps colour it and send it home with a cryptic message like:- 'Dear Dad, I am well and everything is fine. George.' Usually though I had to be reminded most forcibly to send some real news home, but life was for living and most of the time there were not enough hours in the day to cram in all that I wished to do. I have been told of evacuees who spent a most miserable time away from home, some being treated like slaves or lackeys by their hosts, but I must state that to my knowledge none were treated so in Rhymney. Certainly I was treated as a member of the Pritchard family throughout my stay with them. I was considered to be a brother to Douglas and neither of us received any preference. To this day I consider him to be my 'wartime brother'.

My stepbrother Ronald had been evacuated to Resolven, also in South Wales and when I discovered where Resolven was I realised that it was near enough for me to visit him. Having saved some of the money received for running errands and helping at the shop, including generous tips from customers at Christmas, I decided to make the journey by bus. This entailed using the local bus that travelled to and fro between Rhymney and Tredegar and there boarding a coach operated by the Western Welsh Co which passed through Resolven on its way to Swansea. At that time several acquaintances said that the Western Welsh bus drivers had a somewhat reckless reputation.

I think that this comment was unwarranted, although my impression of a journey that appeared to be much too fast on narrow country roads, sometimes almost on two wheels around corners is with me even today. Since there were so few vehicles on the roads at that time it was probably very safe for the coach to travel at that speed. Having arrived at Resolven in one piece, I spent a very pleasant day with Ronald, exploring the locality whilst recalling the times we had spent together in and around the Medway Towns before the war. Reluctantly I returned to Rhymney on a coach that evening and we did not meet again until after my grandfather died in 1950. Ronald left Resolven shortly after our meeting and rejoined the rest of the family. They had moved just after Christmas 1940 to Inverkeithing in Fife, near to Rosyth Dockyard where my stepfather had been transferred.

Later in 1941, a Sunday during harvest time, there was a torrent of water that flowed from high ground to the main street and down to the river. We almost had flood water in at the front door but fortunately we were just clear of its flow. This torrent flooded the Cottage Hospital to a depth of approximately thirty inches, the hospital being only a few feet above normal river water level. An SOS for help to clear up after the water had subsided was answered in part by pupils of the Lawn School and I remember helping with other boys and girls with mop, bucket and various cleaning materials in scrubbing the floors in both wards and corridors.

At Gillingham my language subjects were English and German, both of which were studied at Sandwich and for a short while at Rhymney, but for a reason that I cannot now recall German was replaced with French. It certainly was not because we were at war with Germany, so I suspect that we no longer had a teacher available competent in the language. Some of us took great delight in practising both French. and German whenever we travelled on the local service buses (Parfitt's or Hill's). Often other passengers would converse in Welsh and as this was just Double Dutch to most of us we thought we would adopt a tongue that was strange to our fellow travellers. On occasion this caused some consternation but most realised that we were far too young to be spies, and of course our laughter gave the game away.

For a few months I was the proud owner of two green budgerigars, Billy and Betty. These birds were quite elderly and the correct food for them was quite difficult to obtain. Seed was available but the mixture was not always appropriate. Unfortunately one morning Billy was found lying at the bottom of their cage and about a week later so was Betty.

Perhaps I should mention here some details I remember of rationing. Ration books generally were buff colour. Those for young children under five years and for pregnant women were green and for children of five to eleven years were blue.

A tin of dried milk, equivalent to four pints when made up, was the allowance per family per month. Sometimes dried egg was in tins.

Two packets of dried egg were allowed per ration book per four weeks and cost one shilling and threepence each.

Coffee was rationed so sometimes substitutes were tried; ground dried acorns and roasted and ground dandelion root I remember but I was not impressed with the taste of either.

Like sugar, sweets were rationed, 2 ounce chocolate bars like Bournville and cream filled bars cost two and a half pence (1p) and Fry's chocolate dream bar cost one and a half pence plus 1 coupon. I think the normal size bar used up 2 coupons. Some sweets could only be obtained in particular areas, i.e. they were zoned.

There were tinned puddings available at one shilling each, the contents being enough for three persons.

Flour was usually available but sometimes supplies were a trifle erratic. Whenever there was sufficient cooking fat saved Jennie would bake, usually Welsh Cakes, possibly a fruit pie, and occasionally some bread. Yeast was obtained from the Rhymney Brewery, famous then, but sadly not now in existence.

A typical menu of those days might read like this:-

With Schoolcap, Label and Cardboard Box

	Breakfast	Lunch	Tea	Supper
Monday	Porridge with treacle no milk	Corned beef stew	Jam sandwich	Cocoa and biscuits
Tuesday	Porridge	Steamed fish potatoes and a vegetable	Cheese sandwich	Cocoa and biscuits
Wednesday	Toast with jam	Dried egg scrambled with spam	Spam sandwich	Coffee and biscuits
Thursday	Porridge	Baked potatoes with onions	Bread and cheese	Cocoa and biscuits
Friday	Porridge with milk	Fish and chips (if available)	Fruit and cake	Coffee and cake
Saturday	Slice of bacon fried bread tomato	Spam fritters mashed potato	Bread and dripping	Cocoa and biscuits
Sunday	Slice of bacon fried bread egg and toast	Liver sausage fried bread potatoes and a vegetable	Dried egg custard and stewed fruit	Cocoa and biscuits or cake

On occasions Jennie's sister Betty would visit for the day. She lived in Penydarren in the Merthyr Tydfil area. One day Betty was still with us in the early evening when I came down the stairs spruced up ready to go to the cinema. I was to be one of a foursome of two boys and two girls. I had not said a word about where I was going or who I was going to meet, but it was obvious to Betty. I was only 14 at the time. As I was about to leave the house she called to me and said, 'Don't forget now, keep your horse in his stable; keep the door shut!' What *did* she mean? Arriving at the front door the penny dropped and my blushes were spared, me being then out of her sight.

I am sure that in those days Betty would have been considered glamorous; certainly she always appeared to be wearing expensive clothes, she had very good dress sense!

With Schoolcap, Label and Cardboard Box

Once whilst she was visiting I heard her bemoaning the state of her stockings. All of them seemed to be either laddered or full of holes! Oh, what would she do? With the war they were hard to obtain and of course clothing coupons had to be given up as well! In casual conversation I learned that it was to be Betty's birthday soon, and it occurred to me that if I could buy some for her as a birthday gift it would be a great surprise. A few doors away from the house was a shop that sold lady's lingerie, so bold as brass I entered the shop and asked if they had any stockings for sale. The lady behind the counter recognised me but did not let on and after a brief hesitation asked me to wait whilst she went into the back room store to look. A few moments later she returned with a pair of silk stockings and when I said that they were to be a birthday present she asked me to wait a moment longer. She went back to the store room and reappeared with a sheet of fancy wrapping paper. I asked her the cost and how many coupons were required so that I could go back to the house a few doors away and get them. She replied, 'Forget the coupons, just pay for the stockings.' How much they cost I cannot remember. Later I learned that I was charged only a fraction of the proper cost and coupon free because of my audacity. Apparently the lady thought it very daring of me to buy silk stockings for a glamorous woman! When Betty unwrapped them she thanked me profusely and insisted in kissing me two or three times, with everyone watching, much to my embarrassment. She must have been told where and how I had obtained them, presumably by the lady in the shop, for her attitude toward me for some time afterwards was such that she kept reminding me of my daring to enter a shop that sold lady's undergarments. I'm sure that I was made to blush day after day, everybody seemed to know, even some

RATIONING
of Clothing, Cloth, Footwear
from June 1, 1941

Rationing has been introduced, not to deprive you of your real needs, but to make more certain that you get your share of the country's goods—to get fair shares with everybody else. When the shops re-open you will be able to buy cloth, clothes, footwear and knitting wool *only if you bring your Food Ration Book with you*. The shopkeeper will detach the required number of coupons from the unused margarine page. Each margarine coupon counts as one coupon towards the purchase of clothing or footwear. You will have a total of 66 coupons to last you for a year; so go sparingly. You can buy where you like and when you like without registering.

NUMBER OF COUPONS NEEDED

Men and Boys	Adult	Child	Women and Girls	Adult	Child
Unlined mackintosh or cape	9	7	Lined mackintoshes, or coats (over 28 in. in length)	14	11
Other mackintoshes, or raincoat, or overcoat	16	11	Jacket, or short coat (under 28 in. in length)	11	8
Coat, or jacket, or blazer or like garment	13	8	Dress, or gown, or frock—woollen	11	8
Waistcoat, or pull-over, or cardigan, or jersey	5	3	Dress, or gown, or frock—other material		
Trousers (other than fustian or corduroy)	8	6	Gym tunic, or girl's skirt with bodice	8	6
Fustian or corduroy trousers	5	5	Blouse, or sports shirt, or cardigan, or jumper	5	3
Shorts	5	3	Skirt, or divided skirt	7	5
Overalls, or dungarees or like garment	6	4	Overalls, or dungarees or like garment	6	4
Dressing-gown or bathing-gown	8	6	Apron, or pinafore	3	2
Night-shirt or pair of pyjamas	8	6	Pyjamas	8	6
Shirt, or combinations—woollen	8	6	Nightdress	6	5
Shirt, or combinations—other material			Petticoat, or slip, or combination, or cami-knickers	4	3
Pants, or vest, or bathing costume, or child's blouse	5	4	Other undergarments, including corsets	3	2
Pair of socks or stockings	4	3	Pair of stockings	2	1
Collar, or tie, or pair of cuffs	3	1	Pair of socks (ankle length)	1	1
Two handkerchiefs	1	1	Collar, or tie, or pair of cuffs	1	1
Scarf, or pair of gloves or mittens	2	2	Two handkerchiefs	1	1
Pair of slippers or goloshes	4	2	Scarf, or pair of gloves or mittens or muff	2	2
Pair of boots or shoes	7	3	Pair of slippers, boots or shoes	5	3
Pair of leggings, gaiters or spats	3	2			

CLOTH. Coupons needed per yard depend on the width. For example, a yard of woollen cloth 36 inches wide requires 3 coupons. The same amount of cotton or other cloth needs 2 coupons.
KNITTING WOOL. 1 coupon for two ounces.

THESE GOODS MAY BE BOUGHT *WITHOUT* COUPONS

¶ Children's clothing of sizes generally suitable for infants less than 4 years old. ¶ Boiler suits and workmen's bib and brace overalls. ¶ Hats and caps. ¶ Sewing thread. ¶ Mending wool and mending silk. ¶ Boot and shoe laces. ¶ Tapes, braids, ribbons and other fabrics of 3 inches or less in width. ¶ Elastic. ¶ Lace and lace net. ¶ Sanitary towels. ¶ Braces, suspenders and garters. ¶ Hard haberdashery. ¶ Clogs. ¶ Black-out cloth dyed black. ¶ All second-hand articles.

of the girls at school pulled my leg about it! For some time they kept asking if I would buy them a pair.

For a few days Jennie's father came to stay. He was an 'old sea dog', having served in his younger days on wooden sailing ships. He was taking life rather easily since he suffered with angina. He seldom spoke of his experiences aboard ship but he was fond of performing his party piece. This was to take the large black kettle, once it was boiling, off the fire in the range and place it on the palm of his hand, leaving it there for as long as his audience wished. When he removed the kettle from his hand and replaced it on the fire he just brushed the sooty residue from his palm to show that there was neither blister nor burn mark of any kind on it. For a few nights I shared a bed with him but since I was a restless sleeper, in order that he could sleep undisturbed, it was arranged that I slept with Douglas in Tom and Jennie's bed for the remaining nights of his stay. This was achieved only because Tom was on night shift at the time and I think Jennie spent those two or three nights either in an armchair in the front downstairs room, or on the sofa in the other downstairs room. Incidentally, Tom must have had a very reliable internal alarm clock. He could say, 'I will have ten minutes sleep,' or 'I will have ten hours sleep,' lie down on that sofa in that downstairs back room and without fail wake up exactly on time. Even for only ten minutes he would sleep soundly and wake refreshed.

Materials to decorate with or make improvements to the house were not readily available but Tom did manage to obtain enough tongued and grooved boards to panel the downstairs back room to a height of about three feet. He set about fixing these boards to a pair of battens screwed to the walls, finishing the top edge with a moulding that he planed

William Owen, the old sea-dog. Photo: Douglas Pritchard.

to the required shape. When completed he was unable to obtain varnish stain to coat and colour the panelling. This was overcome by purchasing 'Condy's Crystals' (potassium permanganate) from the local chemist. These very fine crystals were dissolved in water to make a very dark purple coloured solution which was to be brushed onto the woodwork. This I volunteered to do, and I set to work with a vengeance painting the walls purple. I thought it a weird idea, painting the wood purple, but who was I to argue? After having covered about six feet along the wall, I looked back to where I had started and to my surprise the first two feet had changed colour and was now a light brown! To achieve the colour that we wanted, medium oak, I had to repeat the process three, maybe four times, but allowing the wood to dry between each coat to check on the depth of colour obtained. Since the solution was water based the wood then had to be sanded smooth once properly dry because the water had raised the grain and made the surface rough. Tom was then lucky to obtain some clear varnish which was applied to protect the surface. I was told soon after that this same solution in a more dilute form was applied by some of the ladies to their legs to make them look as though they were wearing stockings, an imitation seam being drawn down the back of each leg with an eyebrow pencil. Some ladies even resorted to using light tan shoe polish or gravy browning to achieve the same result.

Tom obtained a small film projector from someone, 9.5mm Pathe I believe, and with it was a single short black and white cartoon film. The illumination was from a low wattage lamp and the film had to be cranked through the projector by hand. Some practice was required to be sure of smooth animation. The characters in this little comedy were a horse

With Schoolcap, Label and Cardboard Box

and a wasp. The wasp worried the horse by buzzing ever closer and the horse tried hard to retaliate by swishing his tail. It ended with the wasp using its enormous sting to inject the horse in the hind quarters which caused the horse to jump right out of the picture, much to the delight of the wasp. Much pleasure was obtained by showing this single film over and over, the show being all of sixty seconds duration.

From the local wireless repair man, David Evans, I purchased a table microphone and a small speaker and much time was spent experimenting with them. The microphone had to be energised by connecting to it a slim bell battery but try as I might I had no success in getting a sound from the speaker other than the odd click when the battery was connected. I did not know that I needed some form of amplification to make everything work. One day, however, I had the bright idea of trying the wireless, which was battery powered, and connected it into the experiment and suddenly, Hey Presto! there was sound! I cannot remember the details of what we did but we were elated to hear our own voices on the wireless. The wireless was powered by a 180 volt dry battery that was quite heavy, and it also needed a 2 volt accumulator which had to be charged periodically and this was carried out by the same David Evans. I believe that there may have been a 9 volt grid bias battery required also. I can remember that my grandfather had a battery powered wireless and that was powered similarly. When the large dry battery would no longer successfully power the wireless because it was low in power Tom would give one of us two dessert spoons which he dared us to use, one in each hand, to press against the end connections of the battery. Doing so produced a shock that made both hands jerk quite violently,

With Schoolcap, Label and Cardboard Box

and if one's hands were slightly damp or sweaty the spoons usually ended up on the other side of the room!

There were two cinemas and both were only minutes away: the Scala, almost opposite the police station and the Victoria Hall which was just around the corner. Many evacuees went to either one or the other about once a fortnight, provided that funds allowed. I went quite often but none of the films I saw then can I remember, but musicals and newsreels of the war I always enjoyed.

More amusement was provided by the acquisition of a punch ball and a pair of boxing gloves. The punch ball was fixed to the ceiling and the floor by strong screwed hooks, with thick rubber cord connecting the ball to the hooks. When the punch ball was not in use the hook in the floor had to be unscrewed from its plate set in the floor and removed since the punch ball had been rigged at the bottom of the stairs. Both Douglas and I became quite expert in punching this ball and no doubt the exercise and improved reflexes obtained from its use was a benefit to us both.

Always I took an interest in what others were doing and whilst living with Tom and Jennie I learned many things. Tom had a first aid manual published by the St. John Ambulance Brigade, which had been issued to him at the police station: he was expected to know basic first aid as a police constable. This manual I found fascinating and in a very short time I could name the bones in the human skeleton, and knew the basic forms of bandage for various injuries. Today I am ashamed to admit that I can only remember some. Jennie taught me the basic stitches in knitting, plain and purl etc., but I never made a success of knitting because I could not keep an even tension in my attempts. Perhaps I should have persevered. Jennie also

With Schoolcap, Label and Cardboard Box

taught me simple sewing, like sewing on buttons and darning socks. With other domestic matters though I managed quite well and the knowledge gained has served me well over the years. From Jennie I learned how to prepare and cook simple dishes and because a lot of ingredients either were not available or were rationed, how to improvise and substitute to provide as much variety in our daily menus as possible. To demonstrate how well I had absorbed her instructions and ideas I announced at Christmas 1942 that whilst the family were at the cinema I would prepare a meal with a difference. I had obtained already my secret ingredient for a surprise sweet course, and I was determined to show off my ingenuity. The main course was something straightforward like meat and potatoes and vegetables, preceded by onion soup. Those details I do not now recall, that part of the meal was a complete success, but the dessert? From the chemist I had obtained my magic ingredient, peppermint essence! This I introduced into a green jelly, using an amount that would have been acceptable if I was using peppermint cordial. I forgot the golden rule – do as all good chefs do – taste as you go, check that the dish is as you require. The taste of that peppermint was so strong that the jelly was simply revolting! This mistake caused me considerable embarrassment, but a great deal of amusement to everyone else. Very recently (1996) in conversation with Douglas he recalled the incident!

Sex education was not included in the school syllabus in those days, but it was about this time that we were given our only sex lesson. This amounted to a brief lecture followed by a question and answer session, the whole lesson lasting fifteen minutes at most. It was obvious that the master intended to get the lesson over and done with in the shortest possible time. The lecture dealt purely with the mechanics of intercourse and the possible result of that activity in nine months. Since there had been no advance warning of the sex lesson, most of us had no questions of note to ask, few of us having gathered knowledge of the subject. One boy asked why it was that hair grew profusely on the head, somewhat less under the arms and at the base of the stomach, but noticeably less everywhere else on the body, he having noticed this to be so on one of the masters when they were changing at the swimming pool. He got no satisfactory reply except that he might get some hairs on his chest later on and if he had not got hair at the base of his stomach then, he most likely would before he was a few years older. Another boy asked if that applied to girls also, the answer of course was YES. We assumed that the girls were subjected to a lesson in similar vein, both brief and offhand, really inadequate; delivered though by a mistress. This was confirmed later by one of the older girls who laughingly added that their lesson had ended with a stern warning to keep their legs crossed and their knickers on, ALWAYS! Navy blue ones of course! The subject was then hurriedly changed to mathematics or some other routine subject such that any questions that afterwards came into our heads was not discussed in class. Many questions did come to mind, naturally, and these were open to conjecture and supposition, and since sex had not been openly nor seriously discussed, or even thought of by most of us, the result was that there were many theories being aired, often in back of the hand whispers and bawdy comments. Behind the bike shed meetings played a part, occasionally in mixed groups I am sure. Compared with young teenagers of today we were really very ignorant of sex and its mysteries. As a result of this brief introduction via that simple lecture, for me it brought to mind an occasion when I was about eleven and at the local swimming pool (The Strand at Gillingham), when a boy of sixteen lowered his swimming trunks and said to the group of boys I was with, all of them of my age, 'Look, if you rub it like this it grows', giving us a demonstration. This occurred in the shower area next to the changing cubicles, and at the time we said, 'So what!' since none of us were really interested. I certainly was not! But now we realised. At the time of the lesson most of us had experienced the odd strange feeling, generally pleasant, a noticeable movement that we thought only happened to oneself, but always to that most intimate place. During P.E. in the gymnasium for example, when climbing a pole or rope and the pole or rope was rubbing the groin an erection could easily result. Sometimes this would happen in class, for no apparent reason, and the resulting bulge in the trousers would make the victim reluctant to leave his desk for a while. Now, knowing what it was that was happening as a result of that lesson, seemed to be making the feelings and erections occur more frequently.

On one occasion I was in a mixed group of eight or nine sitting on the grass in the local park chatting about nothing of importance, as teenagers will, when one couple started kissing, much to the amusement of the rest of us, and the more that we laughed and joked about them being attracted to each other and egging them on, the longer this kiss lasted. When the couple eventually broke free, admittedly rather breathlessly, one of the other girls in the group said to her girl neighbour, 'Ooh! My knicker's are suddenly quite wet!' The boys present looked at each other, puzzled, and were obviously ignorant of what she meant or the reason for her saying it! Including me! A couple of the boys were aroused by

With Schoolcap, Label and Cardboard Box

this kissing episode but did not admit to it until the occasion was discussed later.

I am reminded also of another incident that occurred in the park, this time on school sports day. Since clothes were rationed, instead of buying proper shorts, to save clothing coupons, many boys wore just their underpants instead, and as a competitor in the one hundred yards sprint, one boy did just that. Unfortunately at about twenty yards from the finish of the race and with all eyes upon him since he was leading, his most intimate part, he being well proportioned, appeared through the opening in his pants. This to the glee and amusement of all the girls and boys watching the race. There was a loud cheer, but whether it was for winning or for the exhibition was never clear! How embarrassing for the boy involved!

Most of the older houses in the valleys had a range as the means of cooking and heating and naturally these were fuelled with coal. Coal was delivered by lorry, normally in either a half or full lorry load, it being dumped unceremoniously in the road outside the front door. The whole family would be recruited to fill buckets, tin baths, sacks and any other suitable receptacle, and carry the coal, through the house in most instances, to wherever the coal store happened to be. For us, we were lucky that there was an accessible back gate, where it was dumped, so we did not have to carry it through the house, but we did have to carry it, using the various containers available from there to the storage area under the house. This coal was usually ungraded and it would consist of lumps ranging in size from a pea to to a piece weighing a half hundredweight maybe! It arrived as it was hewed, including dust! Sometimes it arrived as small lumps of varying size in a lot of dust. No matter, the range would burn

With Schoolcap, Label and Cardboard Box

it all. The huge lumps were soon reduced to a manageable size by careful use of a hammer.

Nearby on the mountain there was an adit (a horizontal or level entrance to a mine) and locally it was known as 'The Level' and one morning it was arranged for me to enter it. Although it was an interesting experience, finding myself in complete darkness after a short distance, and having only a feeble light to guide us, I was accompanied by a miner, I found it to be decidedly claustrophobic. I immediately expressed the wish never to be a miner, and I am glad that I was never a 'Bevin Boy'.

Another day I persuaded the Rhymney Stationmaster to allow me to visit the signal box at the end of the platform so that I could see how the signals were operated and how the comings and goings of trains were controlled. At first the signalman made me stand in a corner and watch whilst he went about his job, pulling levers that moved the signals, speaking to signalmen in other locations, either by telephone or by using a code of bell rings. The bell rings in his box he interpreted into messages from those other locations. Every time he moved a lever to change a signal he had a cloth or duster in his hands so that his hands seldom touched the metal. If they did touch the metal he meticulously wiped the duster over it. Those steel handles gleamed as if chromium plated! He said that if he did not keep them clean and polished the oils and acids from his hands would discolour the steel and make them dull. He was obviously very proud of the appearance of his signal box! When invited to operate levers under his direction I found that some were easy to move and others rather difficult because of the effort required. This was because of the length of steel cable connecting the signal with the lever; the more distant the signal the longer and heavier the cable. He also explained the meaning of the different colour lamps together with their position on the front and rear of the train; a different combination of colour and position indicated what the train was, express, slow, passenger, goods etc.

The front gardens of the houses opposite Cross Street had iron railings against the pathway. These railings were made of iron rods about half an inch in diameter and were sharply pointed at the top, and were about three feet high. In 1998 they are still there except that a metal strip is now fitted over the points so that they no longer present a danger to anyone attempting to climb them. In other locations the points have been cut off for the same reason. In 1942 they were not so protected and similar railings were between the front gardens as well, and I recall a very nasty incident involving a black and white dog of the mastiff type. This unfortunate animal had attempted to jump over the railings between two of the gardens but he had not cleared the top and he had landed on the spikes and become impaled on one, the spike having pierced the flesh between his body and his right leg. Seemingly from nowhere appeared a man who managed to calm the dog sufficiently to lift him off the spike and carry him away for attention. This happened so quickly that those of us that had witnessed the accident had not had time to react. I never heard if the dog recovered, but I still remember how sick I felt at having seen that poor dog in such circumstances.

Being nearly two hundred miles away from home and supposedly safe from the attention of German aircraft did not exempt me from being involved in one of their raids. The location I cannot now remember, nor the date, but I had reason to visit someone at their home in a nearby valley and transport difficulties caused me to stay overnight. There was an air raid warning soon after midnight and shortly afterwards some aircraft activity was heard. Suddenly there was a series of explosions followed by a burst of machine gun fire and then a lot of noise that sounded like slates coming off the roof. All of this noise was frightening yet exciting and as soon as the all clear sounded we ventured out of the house and spoke with neighbours. The neighbours suggested that it might have been a German bomber attempting to attack an ammunition train that had passed by on the nearby railway track. Someone said that they had heard a train just before the explosions and they hoped that the train had passed into the tunnel just down the line and that the bombs had missed. Since there had not been any large explosion, this seemed to be a feasible explanation. After a while, and as it remained quiet we all returned to our beds. When daylight came I found a bullet embedded in the bedpost just inches from my pillow!

During the autumn of 1942 I was invited to help in the Rating Department of the local council. How this came about I am not sure but it was probably due to sickness of normal staff or that they were being employed on something else more important. I agreed to help and spent several Saturday mornings transcribing rate payments (instalments) from receipt carbon copies onto the main ledgers. I was provided with a high stool at a long bench with a sloping top on which rested the ledgers. The ledgers were larger than any book I had ever seen, so in order not to damage a page when turning it I had to get off the stool and step sideways with it. Since the receipts were not in alphabetical order it soon made me dispense with the stool because every next entry required a page or pages to be turned. I was warned before I started

With Schoolcap, Label and Cardboard Box

that I must not divulge any details that I might notice, perhaps of someone known to me. For a lad not yet sixteen this was a responsible task and surprisingly tiring: just from turning pages in books!

In the same building on the ground floor was the Civil Defence Headquarters. This was the control room and was connected to other Warden's Posts by telephone. From here the warning siren could be sounded in the event of a possible raid and messages from and to the police and other control points in the area could be received or passed. At the end of January 1943, since I was then sixteen, it was agreed that I could assist in the control room at night and be a messenger to carry information if the telephone should be out of action. This I did on several occasions but I was restricted to nights when I was not at school the next day, so any duty nights had to be either on Friday or Saturday. I had to be accompanied by another lad of the same age and we would be under the supervision of a Senior Warden. Most nights were very quiet and we kept the illumination in the room at a very low level, so allowing us to take a short nap each in turn. The wireless was kept at a low volume also, sometimes there was information of value broadcast, but most of the time there was just music. One night there was a programme of classical music that we listened to which was so eerie that both of us lads began to think that there was an unearthly presence in that room with us. We both went outside for a short while and ran around the tennis courts that were just across the road to shake off those feelings.

One weekend we spent both Friday and Saturday night on duty and, becoming a trifle bored with the inactivity, we spent some time jogging round and round those same tennis courts, just to pass the time, and we must have completed

With Schoolcap, Label and Cardboard Box

*In 1942, Council Office first floor, ARP HQ ground floor.
George Prager collection.*

more than three miles before returning to the control room. Arriving home later, about 7.30 a.m., it was a cold morning, I ate some breakfast and then settled in the high backed Windsor chair by the fire to read the Sunday paper. The heat from the fire soon made me close my eyes. The next thing I remembered was waking, very stiff, still in that chair but about fourteen hours later, just in time for bed! No one in the house had had the heart to wake me.

Another time after a night on duty I went in the afternoon to the park and sat on the grass to enjoy the warm sunshine. In a little while I stretched out full length and in a short time I fell asleep, soundly. About four hours later I awoke, wondering where on earth I was, and what was wrong with my face. I had got a little burnt by the sun. I wandered a bit in a partial daze, very thirsty and with stiff muscles. Home was not far away so two glasses of water on arrival there

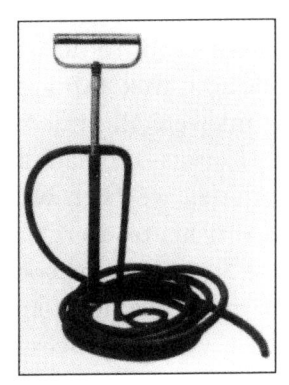

*My ARP Badge, Uniform button and the Stirrup Pump
I was taught to use.*

quenched my thirst and some antiseptic lotion soothed my skin. Fortunately, since it was early spring sunshine I suffered no ill effects.

As I have commented earlier, compared to young teenagers of today, we at the same age were very naive and generally unaware of sexual matters. These days many are sexually active it seems. No doubt there were a small minority that were back in the 1940s, but in comparison most of us did not achieve real awareness until our late teens, maybe early twenties for some. As an example, whilst on duty at the Control Room one quiet night, my colleague and I were both awake and the Warden who was on duty with us was lying on one of the desks and he had fallen asleep. We busied ourselves in preparing a hot drink for the three of us. Invariably this was cocoa, made with cocoa powder and National Dried Milk, to be sweetened with sugar if we had it or if we were lucky with gooey sweetened condensed milk out of a tin. When the kettle came to the boil and we were about to fill the three mugs we turned round to tell the Warden that we were about to make the cocoa, when to our amazement we noticed that although he was fast asleep somehow his fly buttons were all undone and although not protruding from his trousers he had an erection that was fully visible! Fascinated we both watched for several minutes until the bulge in his trousers had subsided. At this we reboiled the kettle and made the cocoa, then woke him to say the drinks were made. We never mentioned the incident to him but the subject was fully discussed with the lads at school during the next few days. Of course we knew that this was something that happened to all males, after all it was happening to us almost every day, often several times a day, but we were not aware that it happened whilst we were asleep. We passed on

With Schoolcap, Label and Cardboard Box

all the details to other boys and we were all surprised at how large a grown man's organ was when it was erect!

One of the local buses that we lads often travelled on, I believe that it was Charlie Hill's bus, a coach really, which went from the Royal Hotel in Rhymney to Tredegar via Lower Rhymney, had a screw head that secured a handle to the back of one of the seats, but this screw head protruded exactly at crotch level when standing. Several of us had the disconcerting experience of having our flies ripped open by that accursed screw when moving from the seat into the gangway. Trouser flies were all button affairs in those days and moving along the gangway of the bus with a gaping fly or trying to do the buttons up on the way was extremely embarrassing. Travelling on that same bus one afternoon I was sitting in the seat close to the window and right next to the platform. At one stop a very attractive young lady displayed her revealing cleavage as she stepped onto the platform. Naturally I was looking at her as she stepped aboard and immediately I became fully aroused, much to my consternation. This had never happened before and I was rather concerned to find that I was still in that state when I had to get up at my stop which was the next one. To shield this state I carried my bag at crotch level as I got off. Now I was discovering how the charms of the opposite sex and my imagination could arouse me, and without conscious effort! Very confusing! Although I am sure that I could have asked Tom and/or Jennie questions of a personal nature about anything, including matters sexual and would have received sympathetic, truthful and helpful answers, I think I was reluctant to reveal that I was ignorant, to a degree, of knowledge of matters so intimate.

At about this time I enlisted as an Army Cadet and I was asked to show my identity card for the very first time as I

With Schoolcap, Label and Cardboard Box

George Prager – Army cadet.

signed the paperwork. That was the only time during the war that I had to show my identity card! I spent evenings either in drills or at the rifle range. Both the Drill Hall and the range were shared with the Home Guard. My service in the Cadet Force was not to last very long as it happened but in just a few weeks I was promoted to the dizzy rank of corporal. Someone said that it was because I was the only one that did not have two left feet. I enjoyed my sessions on the range and had reasonable success at shooting at the targets. One spring evening the unit was sent on a route march. We

My Identity Card.

assembled at the Drill Hall and marched to the Drill Hall in Tredegar, loaded with kit including a rifle. A few hundred yards before reaching the Tredegar Drill Hall we were forced to halt at the closed level crossing gates. We stood at ease waiting for the train to pass and for the gates to be opened. When they were opened we were brought back to attention and given the order to 'quick march', but our legs refused to move at first and we all leaned forward to about twenty degrees before our legs would move. We very nearly fell face downward onto the road.

I have mentioned the pocket handkerchief of a garden. The 'soil' was hardly better than coal and slate dust and was only about three feet by four feet and was between the shed and the fence at the bottom of the garden. Trying my hand at 'Digging for Victory' as a poster campaign encouraged everyone to do I dug this patch over thoroughly and planted seed for lettuce, radish and carrot. These I tended carefully and watered regularly when necessary but all that I managed to harvest were ten very weedy looking lettuce, half a dozen carrots that were just worth eating and a few radishes that appeared to be made of rubber.

During my last year in Wales an Alsatian dog named Judy was taken in to join the household and she sometimes accompanied Tom on his beat, especially at night. She was well behaved and quickly started to be protective of us all, becoming one of the family. I took her with me on walks on the mountain, sometimes with Douglas. Out walking with Judy one afternoon a schoolfriend came up behind me and saying hello slapped me on the back. Judy took exception to this and promptly knocked him to the ground and stood over him with her teeth bared. I quickly called her away, so she licked his face as if to say sorry and came to me. No harm

With Schoolcap, Label and Cardboard Box

done other than my friend having had the fright of his life. Another time a neighbour came to the house to do something to Jennie's hair and Judy was lying quietly under the table. As soon as the neighbour raised her hands to Jennie's head about to use a comb Judy was up and between them growling at the neighbour, but again one word was enough to save the situation.

Writing about Judy reminds me that when I joined the Pritchard family there was another resident that I had forgotten. He was a white Sealyham dog. I cannot remember his name or where he belonged and he was with us for a very short while. If a still smouldering cigarette end was thrown onto the stone hearth under the range he would attack it with his paws and worry it until it had been extinguished. A real fire dog!

In this same year the front room was let to a dentist for one day a week. The room was used as his surgery with the passage on the other side of the partition wall in use as a waiting room. Anyone waiting must have been able to hear all that went on in that makeshift surgery and it must have been nerve racking if the patient being treated had cause to be vocal! There was no water laid on so water had to be carried through in a bucket, with hot water from the ever singing kettle on the range to remove the chill of the cold. The extracted teeth and other pieces of material such as swabs and plugs etc. ended up in an enamel bucket covered with a towel. These were removed by the dentist at the end of the day.

Browsing through school reports of mine for those war years, (found among my grandfather's papers after he had died and tucked away for safety together with some of the cards that I had drawn, painted and sent home), I realise that

With Schoolcap, Label and Cardboard Box

for the first two and a half years my performance had suffered quite badly, mainly I am sure through the upheaval from home and the five changes of address in such a short time, together with a spell of poor health: nothing serious, just a period of being below par, i.e. colds and maybe a little home sickness. I remember that the first thing that parents resorted to in those circumstances was a course of daily doses of cod liver oil with malt, as did Mrs Knight at Pen-y-Dre. This was (and it is available still today) a tablespoonful of a sticky concoction rather like very soft and runny toffee, or like black treacle, but with a taste all of its own. I quite liked the taste then and strangely I find that I still rather like it. Another favourite remedy of the time I recall was Brimstone and Treacle but that seems to be forgotten these days! At that age I was so eager to please that I just had to do everything at a run and this was very evident when with Tom and Jennie. I clearly recall a doctor telling me very sternly to try walking for a change. Attending the doctor's surgery was only at the insistence of Jennie. Thereafter my performance improved during 1942 and 1943 as did my reports and this led to my success in exams at a later date.

It was at this period that, having money in my pocket most of the time, the earnings from the shop and running errands etc. I bought my first cigarettes. It was a packet of Craven A. Except for dearer brands cigarettes cost only six and a half pence for ten: (two and a half pence today). I suppose that as we were grown up (we thought so) we would smoke cigarettes, some boys even small cigars. So I started smoking, which unfortunately lasted for forty years, hopefully without ill effects.

During these years as an evacuee I did receive money from home; usually a postal order for half a crown (twelve and a half pence) and in total I received about four each year I was away. This was pocket money; if I needed new clothes or shoes etc. then the money to cover that cost was sent to Jennie.

Now of course members of the opposite sex began to interest my age group much more seriously. Most of the girls of our age at school were attractive to our eyes, most of them had good figures, rationing seemed to keep most of us free from flab. The school uniform for the girls included a white blouse and most wore startlingly white ones. I suppose this was due to the universal use of the 'Dolly Bag' or blue bag in the weekly whites wash by housewives of the time. I remember that my grandmother would not do the wash on a Monday without one. One girl, Betty, was particularly attractive and being blonde many boys likened her to Jane of the *Daily Mirror*. There were always boys around her, just like the proverbial bees around a honey pot! However she kept most of the boys at a distance for she was no dumb blonde.

Most of the older houses were small and many of the miners cottages had front doors that were less than six feet high. Living in such a cottage in Morgan's Row (sadly demolished some years ago) was my first serious girlfriend Mary. Her father was a miner at a local mine. Her mother was a very petite lady. There was a sister Ann who was married and lived in another of the mining valleys and a brother who was in one of the services. As he was actively involved in the war we never met. By now I had grown so much that I had to duck when I entered their front door. Mary and I were of the same height and she had freckles and fiery red hair but not the temperament associated with it. Mary and I spent many happy hours together, walking and talking and often in the company of other couples of our age. We visited the cinema, walked in those 'Monkey Parades' on a Sunday afternoon, and would sit talking on warm evenings in the park, and quite often the dog Judy would be with us. It has only occurred to me now that I am writing of my wartime years that Mary and I must have had a perfect platonic relationship. We never spoke of anything relating to sex, in fact we did not even kiss each other until we said our farewells when it was time for me to leave for Gillingham. We certainly were very happy in each other's company and we were still a couple when my departure occurred. A few days before I left Rhymney finally, Mary's mother gave me a sizeable package and when I opened it I found a grey suit in a fine check pattern that had belonged to her son. She assured me that it would no longer fit him but it should fit me well and she wished me to have it. On the left lapel of the jacket some perfume had been spilt when her son had worn it to Ann's wedding. I wore that suit, which did fit me very well, on many occasions during the next three years or so and it was a constant reminder of the very good friends that I had left behind in Wales. The occasional whiff of perfume, although faint, reminding me in particular of Mary and her parents. The day that I left, Mary with one of her close friends, Jennie, my wartime mother and a couple of neighbours accompanied me to the railway station to kiss me and wave a tearful goodbye. I was to meet Mary again, but briefly, when I visited Rhymney some ten years later. Correspondence with her dried up since I got no replies to my letters after a while. The visit I made was with my wife very soon after our marriage, and I just had to introduce my wife to my wartime family and friends. Mary had married also, and was then living at Dowlais Top.

The County School for Boys in Gillingham had reopened

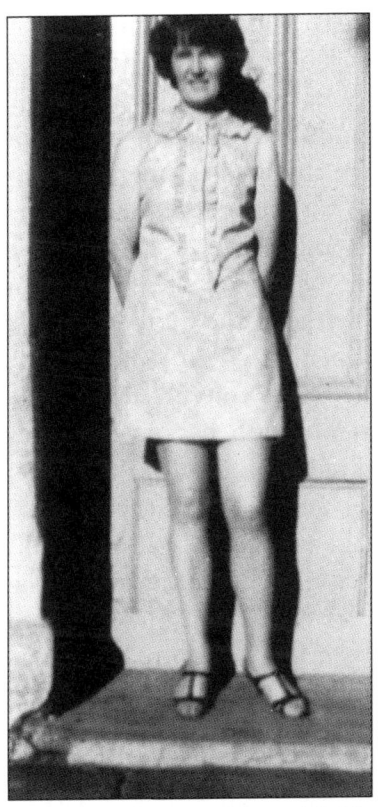

My first girlfriend, Mary. Photo: M. Thomas.

in their own premises in September 1941, and by the end of the summer term of 1942 all of the boys, except myself and two others, Derek Harrison and George Sampson, returned to Gillingham, and the school returned to normal but subject to occasional disruption by air raids and much later by flying bombs. So we three were integrated with Welsh pupils into the fifth form, the other two boys into form Vb and me into form Va which then consisted of seven girls and four boys. The fifth year studies were for those pupils intending to sit

With Schoolcap, Label and Cardboard Box

the Central Welsh Board examination for a General Certificate of Education and these studies were rather biased towards art. Early in that school year 1942/43 I realised that in view of my grandfather's age it would soon be necessary for me to become the breadwinner, so I made the decision that I would follow in his footsteps and enter the Dockyard at Chatham but as an apprentice and so learn a trade. This decision I made without reference to my grandfather beforehand and wrote to the Civil Service Commissioners in London for information. When I informed the School Staff of my intention they were convinced that I had little hope of passing that examination because they felt sure that the knowledge required would be too technical. My mind was made up however, and in due course I sat both examinations, one at the school and the other at Caerphilly. I passed both, each to a good standard. After a medical at a doctor's surgery in Newport at the end of July I was requested to present myself at Chatham Dockyard on 23rd August to select the trade I wished to pursue. I was told that my two colleagues, Derek and George, had returned to Gillingham soon after the school examination which left me as the last evacuee from my parent school. Several members of staff at The Lawn asked me if I was sure that I was not making a mistake and perhaps I should stay on and apply for a place at the Welsh College of Art, which they thought I could obtain easily, but 20th August found me boarding that train at Rhymney Station, bound for Gillingham, carrying that same suitcase and intent on becoming an Engineering Apprentice. That became reality on 23rd August, my first day, and at the end of that week my very first pay packet contained the princely sum of seventeen shillings and three pence. Eighty-six pence today!

So, back home at last, but to air raids and later flying

The Lawn school in 1998. George Prager collection.

bombs (Doodlebugs) and V2 rockets, living almost next door to an Anti-aircraft battery, fire watching at night in the Dockyard, more service as a Warden.

But all of that is, and may become, another story!

CIVIL SERVICE COMMISSION,
NEW COURT, TRINITY COLLEGE,
CAMBRIDGE.

1 - MAR 1943

Sir,

    With reference to your application for admission to the open competitive examination to be held on the 20th and 21st April 1943 for the entry of Apprentices in H.M. Dockyards and/or Artificer Apprentices and Air Apprentices in the Royal Navy, I am directed by the Civil Service Commissioners to inform you that it has been found necessary to make some changes in the centres for the examination shown in the provisional list. Wherever practicable candidates will be examined at the centre of their first choice, but in a number of cases the Commissioners have had to allocate candidates elsewhere. In pursuance of these arrangements provision has been made for you to undergo the examination at Caerphilly.

    Full particulars will be sent to you with the Order for Admission to the examination early in April.

    Candidates not resident in the locality would be well advised to make early arrangements for lodging accommodation which cannot be provided by the Commissioners.

                  I am, Sir,
                 Your obedient Servant,
                    F. L. HOWARD
                  Assistant Secretary

Mr. G.W. Prager.

CONSTRUCTIVE DEPARTMENT,
H.M. DOCKYARD,
CHATHAM.

24th July, 19 43.

Master... P.RAGER...

    Your name appears in the ...33rd... position on the List showing results of the examination for Dockyard Apprentices.

    Will you please present yourself at the Surgery of

J.B. CLINCH, ESQ, L.R.C.P&S,
16, GOLD TOPS, NEWPORT. MON.

for medical examination as soon as possible.

    ~~If you are desirous of a Naval Shipwright Apprenticeship, you must acquaint the medical examiner when you attend.~~

    A further communication will be made when you are to attend for selection of trade.

Yours faithfully,

Schustin
MANAGER.

MASTER G.W. PRAGER,
65A HIGH STREET,
RHYMNEY,
MON.

I WISH TO MARK, BY THIS PERSONAL MESSAGE, my appreciation of the service you have rendered to your Country in 1939.

In the early days of the War you opened your door to strangers who were in need of shelter, & offered to share your home with them.

I know that to this unselfish task you have sacrificed much of your own comfort, & that it could not have been achieved without the loyal co-operation of all in your household.

By your sympathy you have earned the gratitude of those to whom you have shown hospitality, & by your readiness to serve you have helped the State in a work of great value.

Elizabeth R

This message was supposedly sent to all those who took evacuees during World War Two. I hope that Jennie received one.

MONMOUTHSHIRE EDUCATION COMMITTEE.
(HIGHER EDUCATION DEPARTMENT).

RHYMNEY SECONDARY SCHOOL.
("ONI HEUIR, NI FEDIR.")

REPORT for the {Autumn / Spring Term / Summer} 1943. Form VA.

Name of Pupil: George William Page
Age of Pupil: 15 years, 11 months, at end of last month.
Average Form Age: ... years, 3 months, at end of last month.
No. in Form: 11   Percentage of Exam. Marks: C.W.B.   Term Work: 44.2
No. of times absent: 3   No. of times late: ___   No. of detentions: ___
Position in Form: C.W.B.
Conduct: Very good
GENERAL REPORT: Fairly good.

D.B. Short — Form Teacher.

Group	SUBJECTS	Exam. Percentage	Remarks where necessary	Initials of Teacher
I.	SCRIPTURE KNOWLEDGE			
	ENGLISH COMPOSITION		Has worked steadily and has made very fair progress.	h.K.S.
	ENGLISH LITERATURE			
	HISTORY		Has worked more steadily of late	E.H.
II.	WELSH			
	LATIN			
	FRENCH		Fair	J.M.H
III.	ARITHMETIC		} Fair	J.M.
	ALGEBRA			
	GEOMETRY			
	TRIGONOMETRY			
	MECHANICS OR PHYSICS			
	CHEMISTRY		Good	
	GEOGRAPHY		Has made progress	R.P.
	BOTANY OR BIOLOGY OR NATURE STUDY			
IV.	DOMESTIC SCIENCE INCLUDING PHYSIOLOGY, ETC.			
	ART		Good	
	MUSIC			
	WOODWORK			
	NEEDLEWORK AND GARMENT CONSTRUCTION			
	COOKERY			
	GYMNASTICS		—	
	FIELD GAMES		—	

Remarks by Headmaster (in special cases only): We hope that he will like his new work

Date of Re-opening: 16 Sep 1943   193___

Headmaster.
P.T.O.

School Certificate 1943

Date of Birth			Exam number	No. of terms	Age last birthday	Eng Lang	Eng Lit	History	Geog	Latin	Latin	Welsh	Welsh	French	French	Maths	Maths	Physics	Chemistry
M	D	Y				Sa	S(W) Sc	S	Sb	So	Sa (W)	S(W)	Sa	Sb	Sa	Sb	Sc	S	S
4	22	26	Burke Esther	3	15	17	x	y	x	y				x	y				x	
5	27	27	Evans Beryl	4	15	16	y	y	x	y	x		x	x						-
12	13	25	Parman Gwineth Hugh	5	14½	17	y	y	x	x					x	x	y	y	y	
12	21	26	Jones May	6	15		y	y	x	y					x	x	y	x		x
11	25	26	Moore Valerie	7	18		y	y	y	x	y	x					y	x	y	
4	9	25	Williams Ethel Helen	8	18	17	y	y	y	y			x	y			y	y	y	y
7	22	25	Williams Elsie Joan	9	15	17	y	y	y	x			x	y			x	x	x	y
9	9	26	Andrewartha Eric	10	15	16	x	x	x	y							y	x	x	y
7	30	25	Rist Arthur	11	15	14	x	-	-	y				y	x			x	x	x
11	6	26	Williams Emlyn	12	15	16	y	y	x	y			x	x			y	x	x	x
1	26	27	Prager George Wm	13	6¾	15	y	y	y	y					x	x		x		
12	7	28	Griffiths Mary Christine	14	12	14	x	x	x	-	x	x					x	y	x	
8	24	26	Jones Lola Joyce	15	12	16	y	x	x	y							x	y	12	x
11	25	28	Malson Margt Marion	16	12	14	y	y	-	x			x	x			x	x	x	
6	25	28	Prosser Margaret	17	12	15	y	y	y	y			x	y			x	x	x	
9	21	26	Williams Guyneira	18	12	16	x	y	x	x			x	y			x	x	y	
4	3	28	Bignall Glanville	19	12	14	y	x	x	x	x	y					x	x	x	
2	11	27	Brown Patrick Jas	20	12	16	y	y	x	y										
10	8	26	Davies Islwyn	21	12	17	y	-	x	y					x	x	x	x	x	-
12	25	27	Jones Ivor Thomas Noel	22	12	15	y	-	y	y							x	x	x	y
11	28	28	Lewis William Pendill	23	12	14	y	x	y	y	x	x					y	x	x	x
4	7	28	Richards John Idwal	24	12	15	y	x	x	y			x	y			x	x	x	
7	7	28	Roach Keith	25	12	14	x	y	x	y	y						y	y	y	y
7	3	28	Simmons John Aeron	26	12	14	y	x	y	y					x	x		y	y	
9	9	26	Watkins Trevor	27	12	16	y	x	y	y							x	y	x	x
12	17	27	Williams David	28	12	15	y	y	x	y							x	y	x	
7	4	28	Harrison Derek Leslie	29	6¾	14	y	x	x	x					x	x	x	x	x	
12	9½	28	Sampson Geo Henry	30	6¾	14	y	x	x	y					x	y	x	x	x	x
			Supplementary papers						x	x										
Total			No. 5 at Gilligaer City Schools Sittings –		Others 28	28	26	28	8	8	11	11	6	6	25	25	25	8	26
			No 13 at Gill. City Schools 1938 – III		1939 – III															
			· 29		1939 – III															
			· 30		1939 – III															

With Schoolcap, Label and Cardboard Box

What was the reaction of the boys and girls of Rhymney to the invasion from Kent?

Initially, some resented our presence and because our dialect sounded a little like that of 'Eastenders' thought of us all as Londoners and called us such. We soon convinced them that Londoners and natives from our part of Kent were completely different. Some were interested in the difference between 'Men of Kent' and 'Kentish Men', even though there was no discernible difference in the way we spoke. As a result of the relationships that developed between residents of the two areas there were many unions by marriage in later years, also many lasting relationships between families. My own story is a prime example of such an enduring one.

Almost without exception all of those individuals whom I have spoken to when visiting the valleys have warm memories of our invasion, now almost sixty years ago. As an example I include a portion of a letter written to me by a resident of Rhymney today which I think sums up those memories.

Bryn Seion Street
Rhymney
10 April 1996

Dear George,
... George Prager came to Rhymney as an evacuee from Gillingham in Kent and lived at Pen-y-Dre. I remember that there were lots of boys who came to Rhymney from Gillingham to avoid the Luftwaffe raids during the dark days of World War Two.

As a boy of fourteen I worked at Peglers Stores in the High Street and remember the lads from Gillingham walking in the sunshine with big smiles on their faces and immaculately

With Schoolcap, Label and Cardboard Box

dressed on their way to the Lawn secondary school. They were well mannered and always respectful. On Sunday nights I followed our usual custom of going to chapel to listen to some brilliant sermons, (in Welsh of course). Two Gillingham lads came to our chapel on a regular basis and always sat in the front seat in the upstairs gallery. We all thought it remarkable to see them in the House of God yet they could not understand our native language! What their names were I shall never know.

Fifty-eight years have now passed, but we still remember them. The boys of Gillingham, we salute you.

Idris Owen

George Prager – back at Gillingham, 1944.

The 'Wartime Brothers' in 1998.

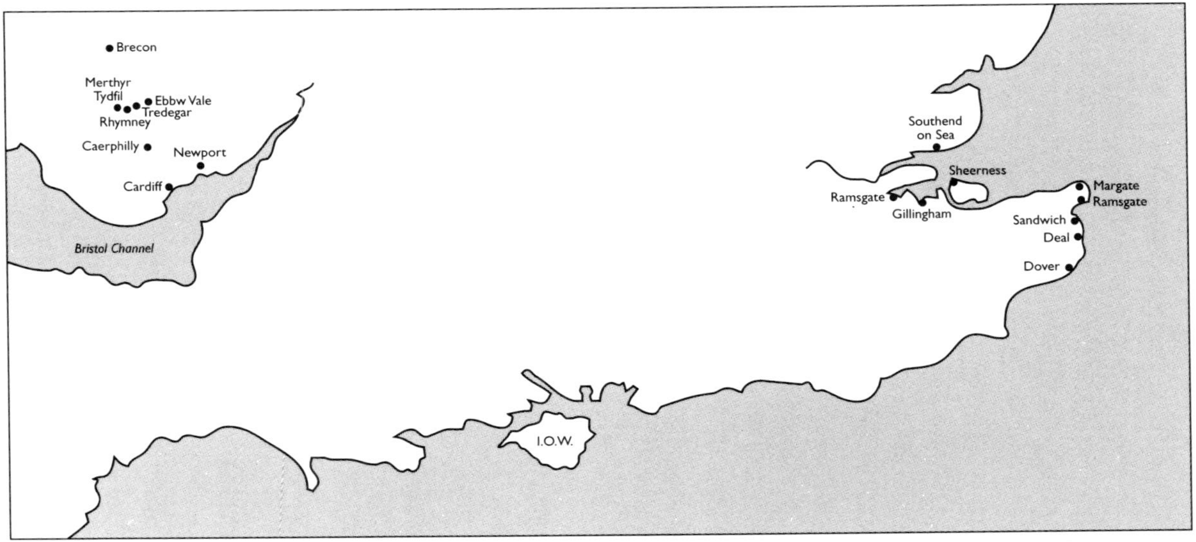

Sketch map showing places mentioned during this account.